The Living Code

THE
LIVING
CODE

EMBEDDING ETHICS
INTO THE CORPORATE DNA

Muel Kaptein

Routledge
Taylor & Francis Group

LONDON AND NEW YORK

First published 2008 by Greenleaf Publishing Limited

Published 2017 by Routledge
2 Park Square, Milton Park, Abingdon, Oxon OX14 4RN
711 Third Avenue, New York, NY 10017, USA

Routledge is an imprint of the Taylor & Francis Group, an informa business

Copyright © 2008 Taylor & Francis

Cover by LaliAbril.com

British Library Cataloguing in Publication Data:
    Kaptein, Muel
        The living code : embedding ethics into the corporate DNA
        1. Business ethics   2. Corporate culture
        I. Title
        174.4

        ISBN-13: 9781906093143 (pbk)

Contents

List of figures and tables

Tables

1

What does a code say?

A business code says a lot . . .
A business code says nothing . . .

Which statement is true?

This book argues that both statements are true. Indeed, a code says a lot, but at the same time, it says absolutely nothing! It says a lot in theory, but it does not say anything about practice. It says a lot about the desired situation, but it does not say anything about the current situation. It says a lot about how things should be, but it says nothing about how things actually are. And because a code says much and nothing at the same time, it is of utmost importance for organisations not only to have a good code, but also to embed it properly.

An ever-increasing number of organisations are adopting a code. An ever-increasing number also have a reasonable-to-good code. And increasingly organisations are also paying attention to the way in which the code is embedded. Three cheers for that! Still, the value of a code is often underestimated. Nothing more than a few communication efforts, an e-learning module and an ethics hotline are employed. And then the code dies a slow death.

This book shows that the code is an instrument rich in potential—very rich even. It also shows that, to utilise its potential, life has to be breathed into a code. But how do you do that? What does it require? And when can you speak of a 'living code'? These questions are the focus of this book.

A code says a lot!

A business code says a lot. It not only sets down the rules of the game for doing business by translating relevant laws and regulations in a clear and accessible manner, but also often sets out how to engage with each other as managers and employers, what we may expect of each other and for what we can hold each other accountable. But a business code can contain a lot more. It may also articulate the ultimate objective of the organisation, the organisation's responsibilities towards stakeholders as well as the core values of the organisation. A good code captures the goals of the organisation (its mission and vision), what the organisation wants to mean to others (its responsibilities towards stakeholders) and what drives the organisation (its core values). In short, a code describes who and what the organisation is or, at least, wants to be.

An ever-increasing number of organisations are discovering the value of a code and are adopting such a document. Of the 200 largest organisations in the world, more than 80% currently has a code. And an ever-larger number of smaller organisations also have a code or are in the process of developing one. While in the 1970s and 1980s companies had to explain why they had a code, today they are cross-examined if they don't have one. A company has to have very good arguments to convince others that it can do without a code.

As a passionate collector of codes—and everything resembling them— my filing cabinets are bulging with the great variety of codes that exist worldwide. From business codes of no more than one page to complete books of as much as 80 pages. From sober black-and-white copied documents held together by a simple staple to full-colour, photo-rich, hardback glossies complete with flourishing golden lettering. From lists of simple *dos* and *don'ts* to highfalutin sentences not unbecoming to a literary essay or a philosophical treatise. And from codes that articulate the norms and rules for using company resources, confidential information and giving and receiving gifts to codes that articulate the ambition to be socially responsible, a front-runner in environmental sustainability and an advocate of international human rights.

A code therefore says a great deal. It articulates the commitment and conduct an organisation expects of managers and employees. And it articulates what others can expect of the organisation. It tells us what the organisation stands for and aspires to: what distinguishes it and makes it unique. And how much energy is invested in its design.

A code says nothing!

But what does a code really say? What does it mean? What does it tell us about the actual state of affairs? Illustrative of the answer to these questions is the following introduction to a brilliant 64-page code. The introduction, in which the name of the company is replaced by **XXX** and the name of the CEO by **YYY**, can be seen in the box overleaf.

This introduction says a lot. The indisputable importance of honesty, morality and compliance permeates the text. It is important for the company to have a highly regarded and respected reputation. It is not to be tampered with. Everyone is to fully comply with the code. And everyone also means everyone who works for the company and has an impact on the reputation of the company. That the CEO signed the code emphasises his personal endorsement: that the code also applies to the most senior person in the company. The tone at the top is unambiguous: 'Let's keep that reputation high!'

There is, however, also another side to this pleasing text; at the same time the introduction and the rest of the code also says nothing because this is, or rather was, the code of an organisation where fraud and embezzlement took place on a large scale. Where, at the time that this code was in force, gross violations of rules and regulations were the order of the day. The object of our attention here is the introduction to the code of . . . **Enron**, the American energy group which in 2001—only one year after the code was launched!—went bankrupt as a result of the gross violation of all forms of honesty, morality and compliance. As a result of the

INTRODUCTION

As officers and employees of XXX, its subsidiaries, and its affiliated companies, we are responsible for conducting the business affairs of the companies in accordance with all applicable laws and in a moral and honest manner.

To be sure that we understand what is expected of us, XXX has adopted certain policies, with the approval of the Board of Directors, which are set forth in this book. I ask that you read them carefully and completely and that, as you do, you reflect on your past actions to make certain that you have complied with the policies. It is absolutely essential that you fully comply with these policies in the future. If you have any questions, talk them over with your supervisor, manager, or XXX's legal counsel.

We want to be proud of XXX and to know that it enjoys a reputation of fairness and honesty and that it is respected. Gaining such respect is one aim of our advertising and public relations activities, but no matter how effective they may be, XXX's reputation finally depends on its people, on you and me. Let's keep that reputation high.

July 1, 2000
YYY, CEO

accounting fraud, shareholders lost tens of billions of dollars. And CEO Kenneth Lay, signatory to the introduction, was convicted of fraud and conspiracy. He was never sentenced as he died of a heart attack shortly before he was due to appear in court.

What do codes mean if their content could be in such sharp contrast with what takes place in practice? Little or nothing, one could say. Sceptics argue that the code says all the more, albeit in the negative sense: the more impressive a code, the greater the chance that it is a cover-up for questionable practices. It is after all in the interest of fraudulent and corrupt companies to develop a good code in order to keep up appearances and keep critical journalists, shareholders and politicians at bay. The more economical a company is with the truth internally, the fewer scruples it has in distorting reality in its code.

After the collapse of Enron, the code turned out to have some value after all. Not only did it provide additional reasons to convict the perpetrators for breaching company policy, but it also even generated an income. The unused (!) codes were sold as *collectors' items* for US$200 apiece at an auction.

The importance of embedding

Does this mean that we should abolish codes because ultimately they say nothing? This book is an appeal against throwing in the towel. On the contrary, even. The more highbrow and ambitious a code, the more work there is to do. Codes are important. Even more important than is often thought.

But a code *as such* is not sufficient. After all, anything may be put on paper. If a code is to be effective, it has to be introduced (to focus attention on it), implemented (to integrate it into the processes of the organisation), internalised (to convince hearts and minds of management and employees) and institutionalised (to monitor and maintain the code and its effectiveness). The effectiveness of a code is determined by its content and the manner in which it is embedded:

$$\text{Effectiveness} = \text{Content} \times \text{Embedding}$$

There are, as depicted in Table 1.1, roughly four outcomes for this formula.

First, there is the possibility of a bad code that is badly embedded. The code would then be most ineffective. The greatest shortcoming would be the bad quality of the code. One advantage is the limited damage it would inflict, as embedding it badly would have little or no impact on the conduct of managers and employees. It does, however, pose the risk of eliciting indignation or protest if the code becomes available externally. At the same time, the storm will die down rather quickly when it becomes apparent that the code is a dead letter and therefore of little or no influence. The advantage of a bad code is that a company is not likely to be accused of

No code: Risky and missed opportunity	Bad embedding: Dead code	Good embedding: Living code
Bad content	**1** Ineffective	**3** Counterproductive
Good content	**2** Counterproductive	**4** Effective

TABLE 1.1 Four possibilities of Effectiveness = Content × Embedding

pretending to appear better than it is in reality. With a bad code the proverbial dirty laundry is hung out to the public right from the start.

Second, there is the possibility of a good code that is badly embedded. Such a code is also a dead letter and therefore in the first instance ineffective. Shortly after its distribution, it disappears in the desk drawer, shredder or 'finalised' tray and no one bothers about it. It may even have a counterproductive effect if people see through it and regard the code as a façade, containing empty promises and creating false expectations, or even as cunning and guile. As more companies adopt a code, more attention is paid to the manner in which it is introduced, implemented, internalised and institutionalised. Having a code is no longer a distinguishing feature. Companies that do not embed the code properly or at all are increasingly the object of criticism. The risk therefore increases that the code is used against the organisation. As a PR director once said: 'The code has become the sword on which we as an organisation have fallen.'[1]

---

1   All quotes and examples in this book are real. Due to the sensitivity of the information, most quotes and examples have been anonymised at the request of the companies concerned. The quotes and examples contain only those facts for which I received sufficient evidence from the companies.

Third, a bad code can be embedded well. This is a dangerous situation that can also be counterproductive, especially if the code is bad in the sense that it prescribes conduct that is morally questionable. In this case, an organisation invests a lot of time and energy on the embedding of a code, but it prescribes unacceptable behaviour. It is like a motorist being well under way, only he or she is driving in the wrong direction. Kilometres are clocked up rapidly but the desired destination recedes ever further in the background. In this respect, a good code that is badly embedded or not at all remains preferable to the good embedding of a bad code.

Fourth, there is the possibility of a good code that is properly embedded. The organisation not only has a good code, but has also introduced, implemented, internalised and institutionalised it well. In this situation, the best situation, the code is effective.

Once an organisation has adopted a code, it cannot avoid ensuring (a) that it is a good code; and (b) that it is well embedded. Abolishing a code is often no option given the many questions it will raise about what the organisation actually stands for. For this reason, adopting a code is an irreversible process. There is no turning back. But, by having a code, the risks increase that the organisation acts in a manner that is at odds with its own statements and commitments—that its code turns against it. To utilise the potential of a code therefore carries a greatest risk. There is nevertheless nothing unusual about this. To reach the summit of the mountain, one has to overcome the risks along the way. And, once one has reached the top, the risk of coming tumbling down is also at its greatest.

The central question therefore is how to embed a good code well. How does one do that? What are the requirements? What contribution can I make as manager or employee? And when is this achieved? In other words, when can we speak of a living code as opposed to a dead letter? When do I know that our code is good enough to be sure that it will be effective and not counterproductive when embedded? And how do I avoid slipping into a counterproductive situation once a good code has been embedded well?

Pressing questions

Embedding a code is not a sinecure. It is in fact rather difficult and filled with risks of failure. The introduction of a code is, by using all its trimmings—such as films, role-plays, e-learning programmes and dilemma games—usually not that complex. Keeping the code alive and preventing it from dying a quick or quiet death is often much more challenging in practice.

What challenges do managers face in embedding a code? The following ten challenges are experienced in practice:

1. It is hard to translate a code into strategic decisions and concrete policy: How do I apply the code in daily decision-making?

2. It is hard to convince those who are fervently opposed to the code of its value: How do I deal with resistance or even outright rebellion against the code?

3. It is a challenge not only to communicate the content of a code, but especially to motivate employees to observe it and to equip them with the skills to uphold it and resolve their dilemmas: How do I ensure that I and others can also comply with the code?

4. It is hard to hold each other to account with respect to compliance with the code: How do I ensure social control with respect to the code?

5. Monitoring compliance with the code is complex: How do I know that we are observing the code?

6. It is difficult to repeatedly ask employees to pay attention to the code: How do I keep our focus on the code?

7. As manager it is especially difficult to continually exhibit dedication to the code: How do I consistently demonstrate the importance of the code?

8. It is difficult to communicate to outsiders that the organisation takes the code seriously: How do I convince outsiders that we take the code to heart?

9. It is difficult to continuously link concrete points of improvement to the code: How do we ensure continuous improvement of our conduct?

10. It is difficult to determine what, how and when to bring the content of the code up to date: How do we improve the content of the code?

These challenges take centre-stage in this book. First, I discuss what a code is, what it entails and why it exists. Subsequently, I discuss how to communicate the content of a code, how to implement it and how to internalise it. Finally, I discuss how to monitor the extent to which the code is observed in order to make adjustments and to account for its effectiveness.

The code cockpit

Although it is difficult and complex to embed a code well, it certainly is not impossible. But how to do that? A pointer to a good living code—and this book—is the model depicted in Figure 1.1. It should be seen as a cockpit with instruments to direct and be directed by. This code cockpit consists of a wind gauge (left), lever (right), steering wheel (middle) and dashboard (above).

First, there is the wind gauge indicating the direction and strength of the wind. It represents the code-relevant situation in which the company finds itself. This situation increasingly obliges companies to develop and embed a good code. Three factors are relevant, as can be seen to the left in the cockpit: (1) general social developments, (2) pressure of stakeholders and (3) developments within the company.

Second, there is the lever. Driving only makes sense when you step on the gas. Without energy, progress cannot be made. The lever represents the time, money and resources that an organisation invests in the development and introduction of a code and in keeping it alive.

Third, there is the steering wheel. The wheel consists of three components. The heart of the wheel is the code itself. This is the point of depar-

FIGURE 1.1 The code cockpit

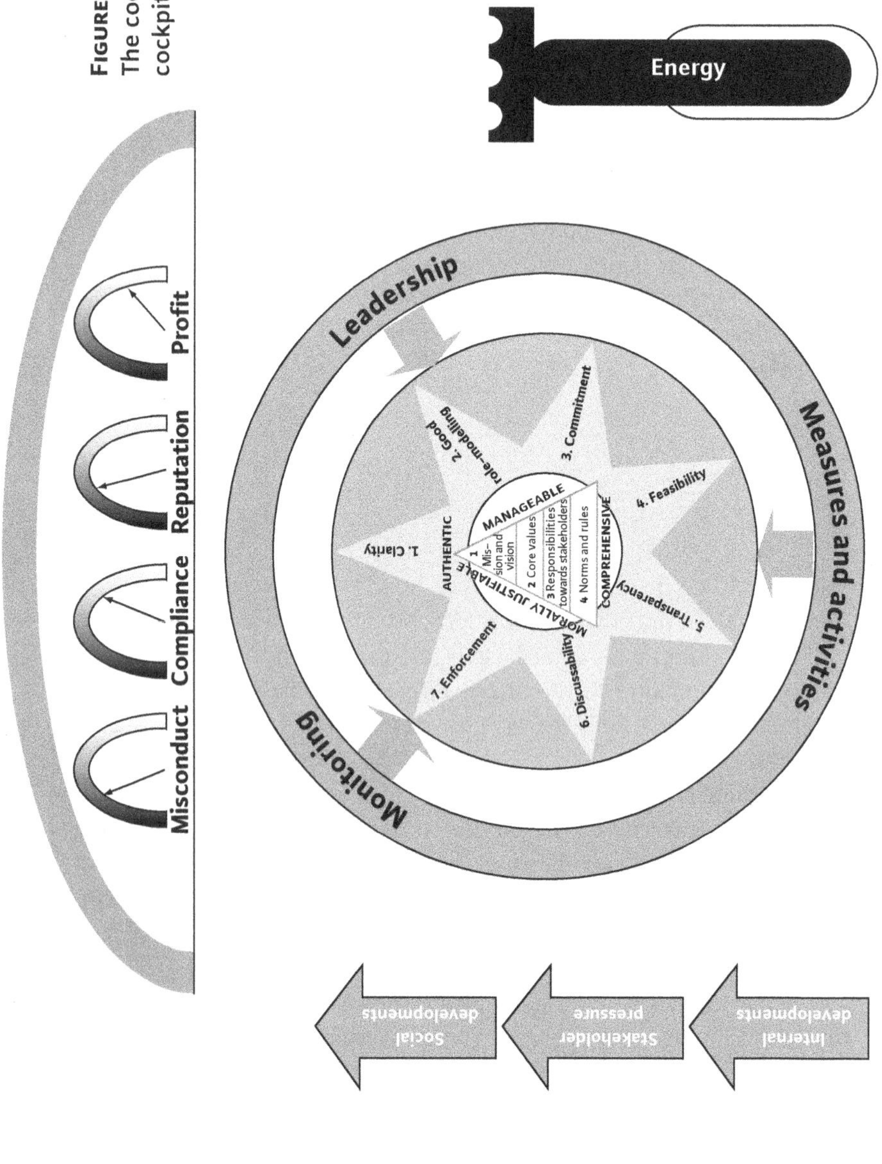

ture for the embedding of the code as well as this book. Codes can be analysed with reference to four interlinked layers in the shape of a pyramid: (1) mission and vision, (2) core values, (3) responsibilities towards stakeholders and (4) norms and rules. A good code meets at least four requirements: it is (1) comprehensive, (2) morally justifiable, (3) authentic and (4) manageable. An excellent code is also morally progressive: the organisation is a front- runner in new principles and standards and thus sets an example for other organisations.

A star is shaped around the heart of the wheel. This code star depicts the necessary conditions within an organisation for a living code. A code is alive when: (1) managers and employees understand what it means (clarity); (2) a good example is set by role models within the organisation (good role-modelling behaviour); (3) managers and employees support the code (commitment); (4) the code can be realised in practice (feasibility); (5) violations of the code are visible (transparency); (6) questions regarding the application and observance of the code can be raised (discussability); and (7) violations are punished and compliance rewarded (enforcement).

The edge of the wheel, where the hands are placed to drive, consists of three handles. These handles are the instruments by means of which the seven conditions above are optimised. First, leadership is of importance: vision, persuasiveness and decisiveness to realise these seven conditions for a living code. Second, a diverse range of measures and activities must be undertaken to embed the code in the organisation. Training, for example, is a means to enhance clarity and discussability. Third, it is important to monitor the embeddedness and effectiveness of the code: to this end, applicable performance indicators should be developed.

Finally, there is the dashboard. Ultimately the code is to have an impact. Four meters are relevant in this regard. An effective code leads to fewer incidents, more desirable conduct, an enhanced reputation among stakeholders and improved financial performance. When you look outside from your cockpit, this should also be visible. You will prosper increasingly. The landscape will become more beautiful. The journey will become increasingly enjoyable. It is, therefore, sensible to map out the correct route and set it down in an implementation plan.

The code cockpit is discussed in greater detail in Chapter 11 with reference to an organisation that uses such a cockpit not only as a management instrument but also as a measurement instrument.

The structure of the remainder of this book is as follows:

- Chapter 2, 'The code pyramid', discusses the nature of a business code and its constituents

- Chapter 3, 'Thou shalt have a code', discusses the reasons why organisations develop a code

- Chapter 4, 'The multifaceted code', discusses the different functions of a business code

- Chapter 5, 'The excellent code', discusses the components of a good and even excellent code

- Chapter 6, 'The nightmare code', discusses the mistakes and pitfalls in embedding a code

- Chapter 7, 'The code star', elaborates on the preconditions within an organisation for observing the code

- Chapter 8, 'Leadership, leadership and leadership again', discusses the leadership qualities required to establish the preconditions for observing the code

- Chapter 9, 'Measures and activities to keep a code alive', gives an overview of the different ways of embedding a code within an organisation

- Chapter 10, 'How effective is our code?', discusses different indicators and methods to measure the effectiveness of a code

- Chapter 11, 'Personal accounts', of three business people on the meaning that a business code had for them

- Chapter 12, 'Leadership once more', concludes this book by naming some distinguishing characteristics of leaders who have succeeded in making a sustainable success of their codes

The cockpit, we learn from practice, offers a sufficient sense of direction and grip to enliven and keep your code alive. At the same time, a cockpit, just like a code and this book, is empty. It only comes to life when you set to work with it in practice, translate it to your own circumstances and develop your own approach from it. As one director tellingly remarked: 'A whole world opened up to me when I finally understood just how important a code is.' On a living code . . . fasten your seatbelts!

FROM THEORY TO PRACTICE

1. What in your opinion does your organisation's code say? How much does the code mean to your organisation?

2. What in your opinion does the code of your organisation *not* say? What does the code *not* mean?

3. If you were to make the effectiveness calculation of your current code, what is the result (content multiplied by embeddedness)? In other words: in which cell of Table 1.1 does your organisation currently find itself?

4. Which of the ten challenges in embedding a code do you recognise? Which are the most important to you?

5. Which of these ten challenges are unrecognisable to you? Is this because they have been overcome or rather that they are a blind spot?

2

The code pyramid

Developing and embedding a business code begins with the question of what precisely a business code is. What is it and what is it not? What does a business code consist of? What types of business code are there? And what is the relation between a business code and other internal and external codes? These questions are the topic of this chapter. The question for you is what type of code does your company have, or, if you do not have one as yet, what type of code should your company have?

Definition

As noted in the previous chapter, many companies have a business code. No less than 86% of the 200 largest organisations in the world have a code. Of those companies, all North American companies have a business code while 52% of the Asian companies and 80% of the European companies have a code. Research per country also shows how widespread business codes are. In South Africa 71% of the largest thousand organisations have a code. Of the 800 largest companies in India, 78% have a code. In the Netherlands, 75% of the 100 largest organisations have a code. And in America, 57% of organisations with a workforce of 200 people or more have a code.[2]

The titles companies give their codes are very diverse. Siemens calls its code 'Siemens Business Conduct Guidelines', DaimlerChrysler calls it 'General Principles', Axa calls it 'Axa Compliance and Ethics Guide', Procter & Gamble calls it 'Purpose, Values and Principles', UPS calls it 'UPS Code of Business Conduct', Enel calls it 'Code of Ethics' and HP calls it 'HP Standards of Business Conduct'. Notable titles are 'Leading with Integrity' of Sprint Nextel, 'Making the Right Choices' of Prudential and 'The Fujitsu Way' of Fujitsu. As we will see, the title of a code often reflects content.

In academic literature, the business code is also referred to by different names. These include:

- Business principles
- Business standards
- Credo
- Deontological code (common especially in Belgium)
- Code of conduct
- Code of ethics
- Code of integrity
- Code of practice
- Declaration
- Philosophy
- Policy principles

What do these documents have in common? When can we speak of a business code? In relatively simple terms, a business code can be defined as follows:

---

2   To make the text as accessible as possible, no reference is made to scientific literature.

> A business code is an independent document which has been developed for and by an organisation to guide the current and future conduct of its managers and employees.

Let us pause for a moment at the most important elements of this definition.

First a business code is *prescriptive*. It describes desirable conduct. It is not—or not merely—a description of existing conduct. A code is by definition prescriptive. A code aims to guide, influence and direct. If, for example, a code states that 'We engage with the environment in a responsible manner', it means that its users are expected to engage with the environment in a responsible manner. A code is therefore not optional. Negating this is the greatest disqualifying factor of a code. A remark such as 'We will see whether we will comply with the code' runs counter to the very nature of a code.

A business code is a *document*. A code is put in writing. It is available in hard copy and/or electronically. A code can be read and re-read. A speech by a manager about desirable conduct of employees cannot be regarded as a business code, even if these spoken words have a greater impact than all words put in writing.

A business code is an *independent* document. It is distinct, separate. Individual copies can be requested and obtained. A code is, for instance, not an amalgamation of a series of passages from an annual report, personnel manual or employment contract.

A business code is a form of *self-regulation*. A code *for* a company is not automatically a code *of* a company. A business code is part of the organisation. It is the property of the organisation. A business code is therefore developed by the organisation itself. The code comes from within the organisation. This, incidentally, does not detract from the fact that a business code can be imposed in the sense that an organisation may be obliged by an external institution to develop its own code. The content however is determined by the organisation itself. This does not exclude using external advice and assistance in the development of a code. Decision-making regarding the content of the business code remains the responsibility of the organisation.

A business code is intended for *managers and employees*. A business code is the code of the organisation and applies to all members of the organisation. It would be strange if the code were to apply only to one part of the organisation. An organisation cannot have more than one business code. A code for one division, subdivision, region, function or relationship cannot be viewed as a business code. In this regard we can speak of a division code, subdivision code, regional code, function code (such as a procurement code for procurers and a management code for management) and stakeholder code.

A business code is in this respect also *official*. Official in the sense that, in order for it to be applicable to the conduct of management and employees, it should also be established at the appropriate level within the organisation. This will almost always be top management, the board of directors or the supervisory board. Sometimes companies also establish the code by means of a large-scale consultation process to demonstrate the code's relevance to everyone within the organisation. One example is a mail-order company that met with the top 200 managers to establish the code officially and collectively. Decision-making took place by asking everyone to rise if they approved.

A business code has a *durable* character. It is concerned not only with current behaviour, but also future behaviour. A business code does not have a short lifespan. It is not a one-day wonder. It is something that lasts for a long or even undetermined period of time. This does not exclude the possibility of changing the code. On the contrary, a sign of a living code is that it is periodically modified and updated. An example is Texas Instruments which has changed its code six times since its introduction in 1961.

A business code is about *ethical* behaviour. A manual for using a work computer is therefore not a code. In such a case, the company does direct the behaviour of employees, but it does not concern a matter of principle. In matters of principle, there are ethical norms and fundamental interests at stake and they involve human emotions. Similarly, a dress code cannot be regarded as a business code as it also concerns a more practical matter. Such a code does, however, acquire a moral dimension the moment that certain clothing is prohibited or prescribed which conflicts with employee rights: for example, when female employees are prohibited from or required to wear a headscarf.

Finally, a business code addresses *multiple topics*. A code cannot be restricted to one aspect of behaviour as it prescribes the conduct of managers and employees in the broad sense of the term. A code on sexual intimidation cannot be regarded as business code as it is limited to one topic. The same applies for a code merely on smoking, use of the internet or gift-giving. Even the sum of such individual codes, so-called sub-codes, does not amount to a business code. A business code encompasses a number of topics in a coherent manner. Indeed, it shows how different topics are related to each other.

In short, not every code is a business code. In the next section we will examine what type of behaviour a code prescribes.

Four layers of the code pyramid

A business code can be said to consist of different layers that can be depicted in the shape of a pyramid. This so-called code pyramid consists of four layers. The lower the layer the more concrete and detailed the expectations of the conduct of managers and employees. At the top we find (1) the mission and vision of the organisation and directly below (2) the core values of the organisation followed by (3) the organisation's responsibilities towards stakeholders. The bottom layer comprises (4) the norms and rules applicable to managers and employees. These distinct dimensions of the code do not stand alone, but together they form the moral structure and fibre of the organisation.

Mission and vision

The mission articulates in a concise manner the strategic objectives of the company and provides an answer to the question of what the organisation stands for. What is the *raison d'être* of the organisation and what is its *leitmotif*?

Cisco Systems, for example, defines its mission as follows: 'As the worldwide leader in networking for the Internet, Cisco Systems Inc. is committed to helping people from all walks of life benefit from the Inter-

FIGURE 2.1 Layers of a business code

net.' Prudential's mission is to: 'Help our customers achieve financial prosperity and peace of mind.' And to cite another mission: 'Novartis' mission is to bring value to patients and customers through its innovative, high quality products which improve, sustain or restore health. Novartis strives to be the leader in Healthcare.' A mission is the proverbial roof over the organisation or the top of the pyramid. A quarter of the codes of the *Fortune* Global 200 include a mission.

Sometimes a mission is accompanied by a vision. A vision articulates how the company sees itself, others and societal developments as well as the assumptions that underpin its code. A vision articulates a particular world-view, such as 'organisations are an integral part of society', 'the world is getting flatter' and 'our licence to operate is determined by our performance on the triple bottom line of people, planet and profit'.

Core values

Core values are the drivers of the mission; they indicate the motivations of the organisation. Core values form the heart of the organisational culture. Core values appeal to the attitude of managers and employees without explicitly instructing managers and employees in how to behave. In this way, General Motors defines seven corporate values: continuous improvement, customer enthusiasm, innovation, integrity, teamwork, individual respect and responsibility.

In the *Fortune* Global 200, 43% of the companies' codes articulate the core values of the organisation. Values most often cited are:

- Integrity (40%)
- Teamwork/cooperation (33%)
- Respect (28%)
- Innovation/creativity (28%)
- Customer orientation (26%)
- Trust (14%)
- Open communication (12%)
- Professionalism (12%)
- Honesty (10%)
- Responsibility/conscientiousness (10%)

Other values include loyalty, motivation, participation, effectiveness, productivity, cost-awareness, discipline, dedication, courage, harmony and humility.

Responsibilities towards stakeholders

A company's mission and values can be translated into the responsibilities an organisation has towards stakeholders. Some codes articulate the responsibilities towards stakeholders in one statement, such as the code of a transport company: 'We strive to gain the favourable regard of customers, shareholders, employees, governments and the general public through superior performance and effective communications.'

Often the responsibilities are discussed per stakeholder. Unilever articulates its responsibilities towards consumers as follows: 'Unilever is committed to providing branded products and services which consistently offer value in terms of price and quality, and which are safe for their intended use. Products and services will be accurately and properly labeled, advertised and communicated.' Environmental responsibilities are discussed, for instance in the code of Generali Group:

> The Group is committed to safeguarding the environment as a primary asset. For that purpose, the Group shall make its decisions ensuring that economic initiatives are compatible with environmental requirements, not only in compliance with current legislation but also taking into account the latest developments of scientific research and best experiences recorded on the matter.

Nippon Oil makes explicit reference to its responsibility to promote human rights: 'Not be involved in any infringements of human rights by engaging in any child labor or forced labor, in all countries or regions.'

	One sentence (%)	One para- graph (%)	More than one para- graph (%)	Total
Employees	2	38	47	87
Natural environment	10	44	19	73
Consumers	11	41	16	68
Competitors	5	35	23	63
Business partners	10	36	17	63
Society	8	34	19	61
Government and politics	9	35	16	60
Shareholders	16	24	8	48

TABLE 2.1 Responsibilities towards stakeholders in codes of *Fortune Global 200* companies

Regarding its social responsibility, Mitsubishi asserts in its code: 'As a responsible member of society, Mitsubishi Corporation will actively carry out philanthropic programmes in an effort to promote the enrichment of society. Moreover, the company will support efforts of its employees to contribute to society.'

Table 2.1 indicates the degree to which the largest organisations in the world include stakeholder responsibilities in their business codes. It is noticeable that shareholders are included in less than half the codes.

Norms and rules

The fourth layer is the most substantive layer and is therefore also the most elaborate and detailed in a business code. This layer consists of norms and rules.

Norms offer guidelines to employees on the manner in which they should act in situations where hard and fast rules are undesirable or impractical. Two examples of norms are: 'Company resources are primarily used for business purposes' and 'We take due care in accepting and giving gifts.' Norms are concrete even if they still need to be translated into actual desirable behaviour. What are, in these two examples, 'company resources'? What does 'primarily' mean? What are 'business purposes'? What does 'due care' mean? And when is something a gift?

In a code, norms often flow into rules. Rules indicate more or less precisely what is permitted and what is not. In this way, the code of Amsterdam Airport Schiphol stipulates: 'Used paper belongs in the recycling bin and disposable coffee cups in its allocated bin.' And Sara Lee/DE states: 'No gift, favour or entertainment should be accepted or provided or will obligate or appear to obligate the recipient.'

Rules of thumb can be found at the interface of norms and rules. In this way, the code of Xerox states: 'If you wouldn't want to read about your action on the front page of your local newspaper, don't do it.' The golden rule in ethics and in all religions, 'Treat others as you would like others to treat you', can be found in many codes in different disguises: 'Treat customers in a manner you would like to be treated yourself', 'Show your colleagues the level of respect that you expect of them' and 'Treat company resources as you would treat your own.' The danger of this type of rule of thumb is that it leans heavily on the moral conscience of the employee. If an employee is less than morally scrupulous, customers, colleagues and company resources in these three examples will come off second best.

In Table 2.2 recurring topics to which norms and rules apply are summarised.

	One sentence (%)	One paragraph (%)	More than one paragraph (%)	Total
Dealing with information	10	32	42	84
Accuracy in reporting (fraud)	11	27	37	75
Protecting assets	11	39	25	75
Accepting gifts	11	28	34	73
Corruption and bribery	10	36	17	63
Sideline activities	11	36	13	60
Offering gifts	9	25	25	59
Contact between staff	15	33	1	49
Contact with media	4	18	11	33
Utilising time	6	8	1	15

TABLE 2.2 Employee responsibilities in codes of *Fortune* Global 200

Four types of business code

A business code can comprise all layers depicted in Figure 2.1 (mission and vision, core values, responsibilities towards stakeholders, and norms and rules), but often a code emphasises one or more layers or focuses just on a single layer (see Fig. 2.2). If the focus is largely on the company mission or vision, the code is designated as **mission statement** or **vision statement**. If that is the case for core values, it is often referred to as a **values statement**. If responsibilities towards stakeholders take centre-stage, it is described as **business principles** or **stakeholder statute**. We can speak of a **code of conduct** if the focus is on norms in particular. And of **regulations** or **house rules** if the focus is predominantly on rules.

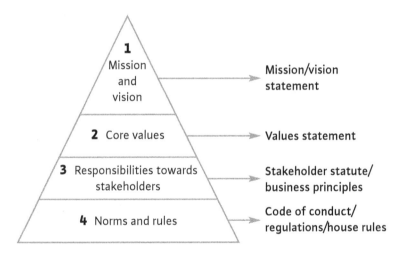

FIGURE 2.2 Types of business code

As mentioned above, some codes consist only of one layer and others of two or three different layers. There are codes that start with the mission, directly followed by norms and rules. There are also codes that consist of the bottom three layers but omit the mission. If a code consists of multiple layers, the sequence almost always follows the pyramid. I have, for instance, never encountered a code that starts with rules and norms to conclude with its mission. It does occur that companies start by naming their responsibilities (outward) followed by naming their core values (inward): on the basis of the responsibilities an organisation adopts, the core values that are necessary to realise it are then defined.

Scope and depth

The question is not only which layers a business code consists of, but also how broadly defined each layer is. Business codes, as depicted in Figure 2.3, vary in this regard from broad to narrow. A narrow code defines its mission tightly, has one or a few core values, describes responsibilities towards a single party and/or formulates a handful of norms and rules. By contrast, a broad code has a broad mission, distinguishes at least four core values, articulates specific responsibilities towards each stakeholder group and discusses the norms and rules on a wide range of topics.

Another important measure for a business code is how detailed it is. A superficial code briefly indicates; it merely gives the broad outlines. An in-depth code is detailed and thorough. Instead of simply stating 'bribery

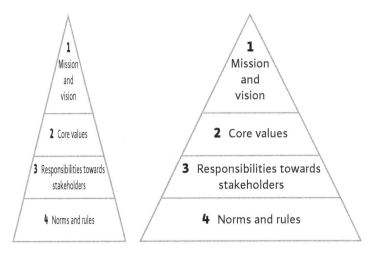

FIGURE 2.3 Narrow code (left) versus broad code (right)

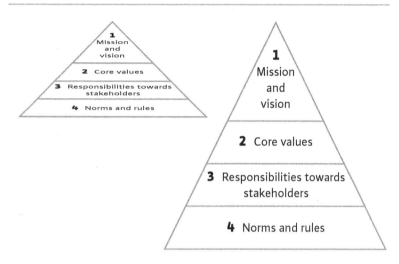

FIGURE 2.4 Superficial code (left) versus in-depth code (right)

is forbidden', such a code clearly defines bribery, its different manifestations and why it is forbidden. Figure 2.4 depicts these extremes.

Business codes diverge as to scope (narrow versus broad) and depth (shallow versus deep). The question is what the coordinates of the (desired) code for your organisation would be if you were to indicate them in Figure 2.5. Does the code address one or more topics superficially (above left: the bullet-point code), or many superficially (above right: the horizontal code). Or does it delve deeply into one or more topics (below left: the vertical code) or does it delve into an extensive range of topics (below right: the comprehensive code)?

Being aware of the type of code an organisation has is indicative of how it should be embedded. In the case of a shallow code, it is important to pay attention to interpretation and translation by its users. In the event of a deep code, it is important to pay attention to the content of the code: there is after all much written in the code. In such codes, it is also necessary to communicate the spirit of the code and the common principles that unite the different topics.

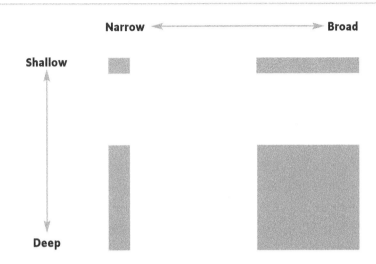

FIGURE 2.5 What is the size of your code?

Translation to sub-codes

A business code that attempts to address everything in detail can quickly become voluminous (bottom right in Fig. 2.5). Many companies therefore opt for individual sub-codes to supplement the business code. The business code formulates the points of departure which, as depicted in Figure 2.6, are worked out as rules in separate sub-codes or manuals for different areas. General Motors had no less than nine sub-codes: for example, for export, the environment, individual integrity and corruption. Organisations that do not have a business code often have specific regulations: for example, for the use of the internet, sideline jobs, security, privacy, insider trading, harassment and complaints. Sometimes these rules are part of the employment contract.

Sub-codes are easier to change or amend than business codes. Sub-codes are often also unavailable outside the organisation and often applicable to a limited group of employees so that the content can be much

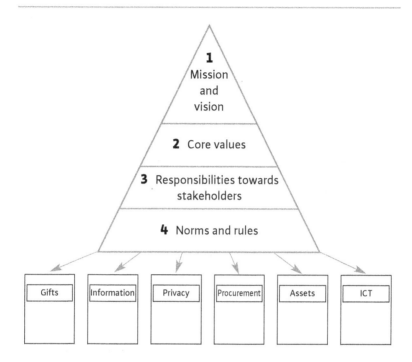

FIGURE 2.6 Sub-codes linked to business codes

more specialised. It is important to ensure consistency between the business code and sub-codes. It is, for instance, very illuminating if links with the business code are established from the outset so that the connection between business code and sub-code is clear. It is also important, of course, that the different sub-codes do not contradict each other.

Web of external codes

Just as business codes can be translated into other internal codes, business codes are often a translation of externally imposed requirements on the organisation. Internal rules on insider trading, for example, are often the result of national legislation. Next to legislation and regulations, other external codes are becoming increasingly relevant to organisations. External codes include:

- **Industry codes.** In many countries a code has been adopted for entire sectors such as insurance, construction, recruitment, banking, pension funds, extractive corporations, weapon manufacturers and waste transporters

- **Issue codes.** In many countries an advertising code, anti-discrimination code, corporate governance code and a code for mergers and acquisitions have been adopted

- **Professional codes.** Certain professions can also have a code such as chartered accountants, procurers, interim-managers, corporate doctors and management consultants

- **International codes.** More and more international institutions issue a code for companies, such as the OECD (Organisation for Economic Cooperation and Development) guidelines for multinational organisations, the United Nations Global Compact, the ILO (International Labour Organisation) Conventions for labour, the rules of the International Chamber of Commerce and the UN Universal Declaration of Human Rights

It is not uncommon for organisations to make explicit reference to one or more of these external codes. For example, in its code of conduct Société Générale asserts:

> Each entity of the Group is committed to ensuring that the rules governing free association and working conditions are respected and prohibits forced labour and child labour, in accordance with the Conventions of the International Labour Organisation, even if such practices are authorised in the local jurisdiction.

Even if explicit references are not made, it is useful to be familiar with the relevant external codes, their implications for the organisation and how they relate to the business code. Is the business code more stringent or are the requirements in the external codes more stringent? Are the business code and external codes an extension of each other or do they strongly diverge? Are they consistent or conflicting?

In short, a business code is often only one of a number of documents that set down requirements for the conduct of managers and employees. At the same time, it is also the most important document. On the one hand, it is the medium whereby external laws and codes are communicated within the organisation. On the other hand, it is the means by which internal rules and sub-codes are linked to each other.

QUESTIONS . . .

1. Does the code of your organisation display the characteristics of a business code? In other words: can your code be classified as a business code?

2. What does the title of your code say about its content? Does this banner cover its content?

3. What is the (desired) structure of your code? Which layers of the pyramid does your code encompass?

4. How does the content of the code of your organisation relate to the content of the codes of the 200 largest companies in the world?

5. Is your code broad or narrow? Shallow or deep? And where can it be positioned in Figure 2.5? Is it a bullet-point code, horizontal code, vertical code or comprehensive code?

6. Which internal sub-codes does your organisation have?

7. Which external codes are relevant to your organisation? And what do these external codes mean to your organisation and to you?

3

Thou shalt have a code

Each individual has a personal code, albeit an unwritten one. That is, each person has norms and values. One person finds pleasure important, another self-realisation. One person attaches great value to loyalty, another freedom. One wishes to serve, the other wishes to be served. Even the most criticised and vilified people have norms and values. The only problem is that their values and norms are not shared by others. A dictator, for example, may strive towards laudable goals, but be despised for letting nothing stand in his or her way.

You too have a code. This code can diverge according to the different roles you fulfil as citizen, family member, club member, consumer, shareholder and neighbour. In your capacity as manager or employee you have a code which guides your reasons to work (mission), what you regard as important in your work (values), who you work for and who you take into account (responsibilities) and what you will and won't do (norms and rules). Whereas some are conscious of their code, others follow it unconsciously. Do you know what the content of your code is? What layers it consists of? And how broadly oriented (narrow versus broad) and explicit you are (shallow versus deep)?

Just like individuals, each organisation also has a code. Each organisation, for example, has values and norms. Often the code remains implicit

and unwritten. The code then forms part of the culture of the organisation. 'This is how we do things'; 'this is standard practice'; 'this is the way
we are'. Such an implicit code is established over time.

Let us illustrate this with an example. Most organisations are offered
gifts and often a specific way or practice of engaging with gifts develops
over time. The following implicit codes can be found:

- Zero option: we do not accept anything and return everything
  we receive immediately

- Acceptable up to a specific limit that varies between $1 and
  $2,500

- Acceptable if it is reported or recorded (and the manager
  approves)

- Acceptable if it can be consumed within 24 hours (incidentally
  applied by a food company which almost went bankrupt due to
  accounting fraud)

- Acceptable as long as it is not more expensive than the gifts we
  give

- Acceptable as long as it does not compromise our independence

- Acceptable as long as we can still face ourselves in the mirror

- Gifts received are distributed or put up for raffle among staff

- Received goods are given away to charitable institutions

- Everything is welcome (as long as it is useful)

Increasingly organisations elect to put their informal and implicit codes
in writing. This is done to establish, and make visible and explicit their
mission, values, responsibilities and/or rules and norms. Figure 3.1
shows the year in which the largest multinationals in the world established their codes. But why do companies increasingly take the leap?
What are the developments that underlie this decision? In this chapter a
diverse range of developments will be reviewed.

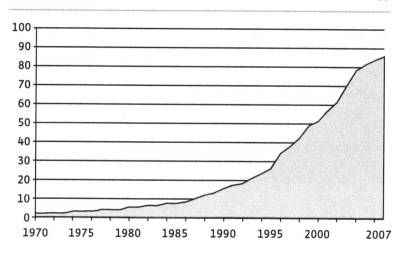

FIGURE 3.1 Increase in codes among *Fortune* Global 200

Concrete reasons

Often the reasons why companies develop a code are concrete. It can be prompted by: (1) general societal developments; (2) internal company developments; and/or (3) pressure from stakeholders. Table 3.1 displays the three different types of reason discussed here. Being aware of the reasons could help you appreciate the value of a code, communicating it and measuring its effectiveness.

Societal developments

In this section, I discuss eight general societal developments that have prompted organisations to develop a code.

1. Societal developments	2. Internal developments	3. Pressure from stakeholders
● Disappearance of self-evident norms, values and social control	● Growth	● Shareholders
	● Decentralisation	● Consumers and business partners
	● Increased misconduct	● (Potential) employees
● Globalisation and diversity		
● Receding government		
● Incidents and declining trust		
● New regulations and standards		
● Greater legal liability		
● More powerful NGOs		
● Increasingly critical media		

TABLE 3.1 Reasons for establishing a code

Disappearance of self-evident norms, values and social controls

In the past, norms and values were embedded in religion and culture. With secularisation, individualisation and the removal of traditional religious and sociopolitical barriers, institutions such as the government and church have lost much of the moral authority they once enjoyed in society. Other previously self-evident social controls have also disappeared. People are increasingly left to their own devices. One of the implications of this development is that companies have acquired an educational responsibility in emphasising, communicating and maintaining norms and values. A code is an instrument that serves this purpose. As one HR director asserted:

With our code we are attempting to restore an ethic that used to be integral to society. As such we are trying to keep at bay the *laissez-faire* and indifferent attitudes of the outside world. We must share the same fundamental moral values from the boardroom to the postroom.

Globalisation and diversity

The world has increasingly become a global village. The world, as extensively discussed in the book, *The World is Flat: A Brief History of the 21st Century*, by the journalist Thomas Friedman, is becoming increasingly flat. Companies do business in different parts of the world and employ people from diverging cultural backgrounds. Multinationals with sometimes hundreds of thousands of employees and offices in more than a hundred countries are faced with the question of whether and to what extent they should adapt to local norms and customs or whether or to what extent they should be guided by the standards of the home country or their own overarching global standards. These questions are raised with regard to issues such as corruption, child labour, wages and environmental management. Companies that apply different standards in different countries have a hard time defending it. In a flatter world a company with subsidiaries throughout the world is increasingly seen as one entity. Thanks to modern communications technology different standards become visible very quickly. For example, in as little as 24 hours a company can be exposed worldwide via the internet for allowing working conditions in its Asian factories that are far below the standards of factories in the home country, the USA. Stakeholders in the USA might be outraged and call management to account for its double standards and lack of integrity. Companies operating worldwide often develop business codes to make clear which standards are universal and to what extent and in which areas subsidiaries are free to determine their own standards.

A receding government

In the past few decades, many countries' governments have receded in a number of arenas. At the same time, companies are appealed to for greater accountability, social responsibility and self-regulation. Companies are therefore no longer able to hide behind government. 'But we do comply with local legislation' won't wash anymore. A code indicates what a company stands for and what it can be held accountable for. As the head of a PR department said: 'Our code fills in those areas that the government is leaving aside or has withdrawn from.'

Incidents and declining trust

Companies are increasingly finding themselves surrounded by glass walls. Tapscott and Ticoll even refer to 'The Naked Corporation' in their book by the same title. Misconduct—real or alleged—is placed under a magnifying glass. Top managers guilty of insider trading elicit outrage from the public. Book-keeping fraud can lead to bankruptcy. Opinion surveys show that confidence in companies and managers is often quite low. The 'Gallup International Voice of the People' survey recently found that a third of the 55,000 people from 60 countries taking part view company managers as unethical, dishonest and too powerful. Companies are also often seen as the source of a number of societal problems. In this regard a code can be a means to communicate a company's disapproval of reprehensible conduct and how it goes about combating it, along with the effort it makes to resolve societal problems.

New regulations and standards

Several international, national and industry-wide organisations develop standards for doing business. In the previous chapter, a few of these standards were mentioned. National governments—despite their receding character—also keep introducing new regulations applicable to business. The US Foreign Corrupt Practices Act (FCPA) is such a law with a very broad extraterritorial effect, which, with its updates since 1977, has had an increasingly great impact on the international business world. A code then becomes an instrument to translate new regulations to the situation of a particular company and to make it accessible and understandable for its managers and employees. In this way, the FCPA is often also extensively covered in codes.

Greater legal liability

In many countries, administrators of justice increasingly scrutinise companies on the measures they have taken to prevent, detect and repress illegal conduct. The level of punishment depends on the degree to which the organisation has taken measures to prevent incidents from occurring and in the event they do occur, to detect, correct and redress them in a timely manner. The American Federal Sentencing Guidelines, for example, take into account whether a company has a code that prohibits a given violation. The fine can be reduced by as much as 95% if an organisation can demonstrate that it has an effective ethics and compliance programme in place. In addition, we see that the personal accountability of managers is also increasing. The US Sarbanes–Oxley Act stipulates that the CEO and senior financial officers of a company should have an ethics code and also publish it externally or explain the absence of a code. In the event of a breach of this code and the law in general, these managers bear the primary responsibility and high fines and prison sentences are not excluded. 'Our CEO's motive for introducing and implementing a code is very important and personal' according to the head of a compliance office: 'CMA, or, _cover my ass._'

More powerful NGOs

Many citizens and societal groupings are concerned about the power and operations of organisations and—with the support of the media—demand that they account for their actions. Pressure groups are focusing less on governments and more on companies. Worldwide there are tens of thousands of non-governmental organisations (NGOs). Amnesty, for example, focuses on companies that are implicated in human rights abuses and calls on them to adopt a code that refers explicitly to the Universal Declaration of Human Rights. Transparency International calls companies to account for their policies on corruption and urges companies to distance themselves from corrupt practices in their codes. Companies therefore develop a code to keep critical NGOs at bay, to demonstrate that they understand and take them seriously and engage with them in dialogue.

Increasingly critical media

Companies are often negatively portrayed in the news and explicitly requested to prevent incidents from occurring. Even if media reports prove to be one-sided or wrong, the damage is often already done. A code provides some protection against the whims of the media. It shows that the company is committed to doing business in an honest and respectable manner. It also sends a consistent and unambiguous message to the outside world. In this way, a telecom company decided to adopt a code after it was subjected to negative publicity on a number of matters. The company discovered that, whether it concerned mass retrenchment, health risks in the use of mobile phones or conducting business in countries where corruption is rife, public opinion was fundamentally negative. In these circumstances a code was developed to launch a charm offensive and to demonstrate the company's awareness of the issues at stake and its courage to dirty its hands should it be necessary.

Internal developments

In addition to the aforementioned more general societal developments, there may also be internal reasons for adopting a code. Three strongly related reasons are discussed here.

Growth

When companies grow, recruit more staff and become more diverse in their composition, the need for a shared frame of reference increases. With this the company articulates its identity. A former chairman of the board of directors of a large construction company described the considerations in his decision to develop a written code as follows:

> In the past I used to say: 'I don't care for a written code; it must be in the minds of the people.' I have now changed my stance. The majority of management feel the need for a code. Our company has grown exponentially. And then

the values and norms of the leaders are not automatically shared by employees. Our business code promotes the establishment of a single business culture.

Decentralisation

Company structures have become greatly decentralised. Many offices and employees have more autonomy but are also confronted with more and greater 'temptations'. Examples include procurers, traders and financial experts who close large and often very complex deals. A code is an instrument by means of which the same behavioural framework is established throughout the organisation. For this reason a consultancy firm decided to develop its own code. While the firm grew large under a hierarchical management structure where all important decisions were made by the partners, the professionalisation of the consultancy profession and the complexity of assignments resulted in an increase in consultants' autonomy. The consultants visited clients independently and started consulting them personally. As a result the role of the partners in assignments became marginal. A consultancy code was introduced in order to clarify acceptable and unacceptable conduct. In addition, the code was communicated to clients with the acceptance of an assignment so that the client could signal alarm should the consultant be in breach of the code.

Increased misconduct

Fraud or wrongful use of company resources occurs in many companies to a greater or lesser degree. In addition, undesirable conduct such as harassment, aggression, discrimination, abuse of power and sexual intimidation also occur. The president of legal affairs of a global manufacturer of consumer goods formulated this succinctly: 'Many people think that fraud stops at the front door. But that's nonsense; we are part of society and just like it occurs outside the front gate, it occurs also inside.' Research by KPMG shows, as depicted in Table 3.2, the different forms and rates of reprehensible behaviour that the American working population have observed within a time-frame of one year. Even if it is only perceptions that are measured and there is much contamination of data, the

Observed misconduct	Rate of observance (%)
Wasting, mismanaging or abusing the organisation's resources	39
Discriminating against employees	38
Violating workplace health and safety rules	33
Engaging in sexual harassment or creating a hostile work environment	30
Violating employee wage, overtime or benefit rules	29
Breaching employee privacy	29
Engaging in false or deceptive sales and marketing practices	22
Mishandling or misusing confidential or proprietary information	21
Engaging in activities that pose a conflict of interest	20
Falsifying time and expense reports	20
Breaching computer, network or database controls	18
Breaching customer or consumer privacy	18
Violating environmental standards	18
Entering into customer contract relationships without the proper terms, conditions or approvals	17
Stealing or misappropriating assets	16
Violating document retention rules	16
Abusing substances (drugs, alcohol) at work	16
Making false or misleading claims to the public or media	16
Violating contract terms with customers	14
Accepting inappropriate gifts or kickbacks	14
Exposing the public to safety risk	14
Improperly gathering competitors' confidential information	13

TABLE 3.2 US workplace violations

figures do not lie. A code is an instrument to combat such behaviour and, should it nevertheless occur, to denounce it and address it. Often companies develop a code after having been confronted with one or more incidents. Face to face with the undeniable facts, the eyes of the board are opened and the time is ripe to ensure that the chances of a repeat of the incident are ruled out or diminished. Even if one locks the proverbial stable door after the horse has bolted the likelihood that more will follow is in any event reduced.

Pressure from stakeholders

In addition to the more general societal developments and the more specific developments internal to the company, stakeholders could also prompt a company to develop a code. In this regard, at least three important stakeholder groups can be distinguished.

Shareholders

Institutional investors have an active interest in corporate governance, sustainable investments, ethical business practices, a robust company culture and strong leadership. In the compilation of their portfolio they increasingly take into consideration whether a company has a business code. Sometimes at shareholder meetings, companies are asked to account for the extent to which the code is upheld with regard to human rights violations, labour rights, child labour and environmental management. Increasingly, shareholders also ask companies to demonstrate compliance with the code. The demand to 'tell us' is being supplemented by the demand to 'show us' how this is actually realised in practice.

Consumers and business partners

Consumers have certain perceptions of products and brands that they value. The identity and image of a company as the provider of a product or service influences such perceptions. A code is an instrument for establishing a sound reputation. And, if the code is not managed well, the reputation of the company can easily be damaged. Increasingly consumers take into account social issues such as labour conditions, animal welfare, environmental impacts (the so-called ecological footprint) and human rights. Consumer organisations are therefore calling for greater transparency on the part of companies with regard to their social standards as well as their social performance.

Also in business-to-business relations, codes are growing in importance. In supply chain management, companies are making greater demands of suppliers, screening them on their integrity or requiring them to commit to upholding the code in the contract they conclude. In this way Nike has been distributing its code of conduct to suppliers since 1992 and monitors and audits them according to a special reporting system, SHAPE (Safety, Health, Attitude of management, People and Environment). And Shell, according to its annual sustainability report, ended contracts with more than 40 suppliers in 2006 as a result of non-compliance with the Shell Business Principles.

(Potential) employees

More and more employees judge their (potential) employer on what it stands for. They want to work for a company that has a clear identity they can be proud of and not feel ashamed of because of malpractices. Their loyalty is no longer a given. A code communicates a company's principles and objectives to (prospective) employees. As one businessman remarked: 'Our business code is a means to attract and retain employees.' In fact, the questions of job applicants even prompted one company to establish a code:

> To our existing staff it was clear how we went about our business. But prospective employees, especially graduates, questioned us more and more on what the company stood for. Without having something in writing it remains difficult to explain. For this reason we decided to draw up a code which articulates our morals and ethics concisely. Now we send the code to each applicant before they are interviewed and we've regained control in this area.

Why no business code?

Still, not every company has a code. In my visits to companies without a code, I encountered the following reactions (also often heard from managers and employees inside the company who question the importance of a code).

'We're doing perfectly well without a code' is an oft-heard reason for not having a code. And, indeed, 'if it ain't broke why fix it?' At the same time, it raises the question of whether the developments discussed in this chapter are completely irrelevant.

'We have more urgent, strategic priorities' is heard just as often. It is logical for a company in the middle of a large reorganisation, strategic reorientation or a takeover battle not to view the development of a code as a priority or to fear that it could backfire. The only counter-argument that can be given is that there are indeed companies that introduce a code as part of a reorganisation so as to set the tone for the future; that develop a code as part of strategic change in order to provide assurance on the new course to be followed; and that introduce a code in advance of or during a merger in order to clarify the new identity and rules.

'A code is not suited to our culture' is also often advanced as a consideration or objection. 'We have an informal culture where nothing is put in writing. Why should we have a code?' asked one entrepreneur. It is certainly true that a code should be related to the culture of an organisation. But perhaps this relationship has more to do with the type of code one should introduce than having or not having a code. It is particularly important in an informal culture to talk about what it is that binds people if a company is not to disintegrate. To establish a code would then simply be to put in writing the content of these conversations. Even if it is only set down in draft form on a scrap of paper, it could fulfil the important function of reference at a later stage. Or it could serve as a means to communicate the culture—albeit in a nutshell—to new employees.

'A code is too expensive' is also mentioned from time to time. The question is whether a code is actually that costly (time- and money-wise). Organisations can develop a code by putting a few points of discussion on the agenda of regular work meetings, and feedback can be used to develop these points further. It's true that, if a code of 80 pages is to be developed and disseminated among employees in a hundred countries and distributed also externally, more work will be required. But in many other cases it can be done more swiftly and cost-effectively. Moreover, investments are not merely about the costs but always about the accompanying benefits. To regard a code as expensive is therefore often an underestimation of its potential value.

'We are too small' is a common objection from small and medium-sized enterprises. In a small company an entrepreneur can communicate values and norms more directly, set the example personally, address employees directly, and so on. In this context, a detailed code does not seem the obvious choice. But also here it is possible to write up the standards in a few pages. The entrepreneur can fall back on this short code and raise it for discussion when required. And it should also be remembered that the smaller an organisation, the more readily a code can be developed and embedded.

'A code is not effective' is, to conclude, another objection that is often voiced. In this view, a code is not the right instrument to realise the intended results. In addition, it can also backfire on a company, as was shown earlier. In the rest of this book, we shall see that a code can be very effective provided that the content is good and it is embedded well.

The conclusion to the above is that not every organisation without a code will make blunders and fail. It is, however, important that companies without a code ask themselves whether they have taken all arguments for and against into consideration. For organisations with a code it is important to remain aware of why they have a code. Putting effort into a code because 'it's there' is not particularly convincing or stimulating.

TRANSLATION INTO PRACTICE . . .

1. Which of the societal and internal company developments discussed in this chapter requires your organisation to formulate an explicit code?

2. What interest does each of the following stakeholders have in your organisation's development of a code?
   - Shareholders
   - Employees
   - Customers/consumers
   - Suppliers/business partners
   - NGOs
   - Governments

3. What are the expectations of the respective stakeholders regarding the content of the code? How explicit and specific are their expectations? And how realistic are these expectations?

4. To what extent do you share the six reasons for not developing a code? And how would you respond to people within your organisation who advance such arguments?

4
The multifaceted code

In the previous chapter we discussed the reasons for developing a code by placing it within a broader societal and organisational context. We touched on how a company's adoption of a code can turn these developments into a competitive advantage. In this chapter we will discuss in more detail what a business code actually does. What are the functions of a code, which metaphors exist to describe it and how does a code relate to company policy? We shall see that a code is a multifaceted instrument.

Functions

With a code, external stakeholders and employees know what they can expect of the organisation and what it can be held accountable for. Conversely, employees and even external stakeholders know what the organisation expects of them and what they can be held accountable for.

A code fulfils a diverse range of internal and external functions. Internal functions with regard to managers and employees include:

- **Orientational function.** A code sharpens awareness of the mission of the company, the relevant values, responsibilities, norms and rules, and it confronts people with worn-out habits. 'Without even having read the code, the organisation has made it clear to us that doing business in a respectable manner is a point of particular importance' according to one employee who had just received the company code after attending a workshop. Apart from the content of the code its introduction itself is a significant signal

- **Clarifying function.** A code provides clarity about the ethic that is to prevail. The code illuminates and explains. This function was clearly illustrated by the following remark by a participant in a code training session: 'At last we know where we stand! The code clearly indicates the boundaries of the playing field and how we play the business game. You now even know when you are offside!'

- **Guiding function.** A code formulates company expectations of employees, guides their conduct and gives guidance. The objective of a code, as stated in the definition of a business code in Chapter 2, is after all to direct the conduct of managers and employees. 'Now that the code is a fact, I'm beginning to realise that I will have to adapt my behaviour. Some practices simply won't do any longer. But a fault confessed is half redressed,' according to one manager

- **Stimulating function.** A code stimulates engagement and loyalty of managers and employees. A code appeals to their sense of responsibility and inspires them to commit themselves to the mission and goals of the organisation. The head of public affairs of a car manufacturer formulated it strikingly: 'Our code is the engine that drives our organisation: it contains so much energy to draw on and propel us forward'

- **Initiating function.** A code stimulates activities aimed at improving the organisation. The code acts as mirror by means of which gaps and deviations can readily be detected and addressed. 'Once we had the code, we just had to. There was no turning back. And that extra push was exactly what we needed'

- **Internal corrective function.** A code creates checks and balances. Management and employees can call each other to account regarding compliance with the code. The code formulates a common ground, a vocabulary, a framework with reference to which discussions can be held. 'With the code on hand the discussion on norms and values has become much easier' was a reaction heard during an audit of its implementation. The code provides a basis for social correction

A code can also have external functions:

- **Distinguishing function.** A code enlarges the recognisability of the organisation to the outside world; the organisation makes known what it stands for. Research conducted for a chemical company into the reaction of stakeholders, shortly after they received the new code of that company, led to remarks such as: 'Good move by the company: now we know what the company stands for', 'When we received the code my colleagues and I were unanimous in our opinion that the company scored a hat-trick: with this document the company distinguishes itself positively from other companies in the industry' and 'The code is very suited to this company'

- **Legitimating function.** With a code an organisation clarifies what it would and would not do and what guides it. A code can therefore enhance stakeholder trust in a company. 'The new code improved our trust in the company: at last it acknowledged its responsibility for this social issue,' according to one NGO

- **External corrective function.** A code creates external checks and balances. Individuals and societal groupings can follow companies' compliance with the code. An encouraging remark of a manager in this regard was: 'Shareholders, but also consumers and suppliers regularly quote our code and ask us to explain our decisions with reference to our code'

The weight accorded to the internal and external function of a code varies by company. Where one company may attribute a primarily external function to the code, another may attribute a primarily internal function. At the same time, a code that has been introduced properly will quickly acquire both an internal and an external function. When a code affects the behaviour of managers and employees, it cannot but become visible to the outside world. A code that has an impact on the outside world will result in managers and employees being held accountable by the outside world and it will generate increased pressure to act in accordance with the code.

Metaphors

The meaning and function of a code can be illuminated through the use of metaphors. Metaphors are powerful images that can be employed to communicate the value and importance of a code. Such powerful metaphors include:

- **Benchmark.** The code is the measure of success; it determines how to behave and perform

- **Business card.** With a code a company presents who and what it is to the outside world

- **Cement.** The code ensures that different divisions, disciplines and hierarchical levels are connected and that its sum amounts to more than its parts (cohesion)

- **Compass.** The code directs the thinking, feelings and conduct of managers and employees

- **Conscience.** The code describes what the company considers to be its moral responsibility. The code is a record of what has been agreed to, an ethic made concrete

- **Constitution.** The code comprises the fundamental rules and principles of the organisation

- **Contract** or **covenant**. The code articulates that which has been agreed to and that to which the parties concerned have committed themselves

- **Cornerstone** or **keystone**. The code holds the organisation together

- **Detergent**. The code stimulates the capacity for self-cleansing

- **DNA**. The code expresses the identity and legacy of the organisation

- **Framework** and **skeleton**. The code is the structure around which everything is organised, the point of reference to which all activities and initiatives can be related

- **Lens**. The code is the perspective from which to examine everyday issues at work

- **Remote control**. The code is an instrument to manage the conduct of others from a distance

Metaphors cannot only express the positive function of a code, but also objections and limitations to it. I once asked participants in a workshop to bring along an object that symbolised their code. I had a great surprise. Someone brought along a brick to express how heavily the code weighed on him. Another brought along a piece of rope to signify that the code was a noose which could hang you at any moment. Everyone was impressed by the participant who brought along a flower. She started by saying how pretty the flower was and how the code appealed to her: colourful, unique and captivating. Then came the 'but'. She continued by telling us that the flower would wilt in a few days and lose all its charm. She foresaw the same end for the code. A better start for a workshop could not be wished for. All resistance was immediately laid on the table. Should you ever be at a loss about how to start discussing a code, asking people to select an object that represents the code is a guarantee of success.

Disciplines

In its most comprehensive form a business code describes what the organisation essentially is and wants to be. It articulates common objectives and principles and thus forms the heart of the organisation. As depicted in Figure 4.1 the business code becomes the overarching vision which connects different focus points and management disciplines with each other. It can turn out as follows.

- **Strategy.** The code articulates the basic assumptions and principles for company strategy on the basis of which concrete annual targets are set

- **Quality.** The code articulates the desired quality not only of products and services but also of stakeholder relationships

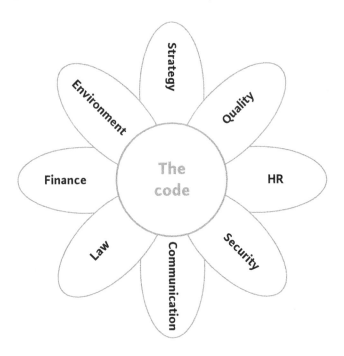

Figure 4.1 Code as connection between disciplines

- **Human resources.** The code indicates what employees can expect and what they need to adhere to

- **Security.** The code determines how employees are to engage with the property and information of the company and external parties that they have access to on the basis of their function

- **Communication.** The code describes the basic principles governing communication (openness, transparency, consultation and dialogue), the manner in which the organisation would like to engage with stakeholders and what they may expect

- **Law.** The code translates external laws and regulations into internal policy

- **Finance.** The code articulates the principles of accounting and reporting

- **Environment.** The code functions as a point of departure in environmental management

The art therefore lies in translating the code to the different management disciplines and to determine at the same time how the code can be employed optimally from the perspectives of each management discipline. Different support staff often have a responsibility for a specific part of the business code. The mission often falls to the strategy department. The HR and quality management departments are often occupied with the values of the organisation. Responsibilities towards stakeholders are often assigned to the department of corporate communications or public affairs. Generally, the responsibility for rules and regulations is spread throughout the organisation. Normally each support staff department sets down rules for conduct which are issued to the rest of the organisation. In this way, corporate communications establishes rules to handle requests from the media, security establishes rules to treat company property, and finance develops rules regarding financial reporting, expenses and accounts. At the same time, legal often fulfils a coordinating role in the development and introduction of these rules and sub-codes.

An interesting exercise in this regard is to examine the code line by line and to relate it to the particular support staff department that has the responsibility to maintain it. By indicating this responsibility per line (or even word), it not only becomes clear what the function of each support staff department is, but also which sections of the code still need to be allocated. In one company where this was examined, it turned out that, despite the fact that the code had been in existence for more than five years, half of it had not been assigned to a particular department even though it was quite clear where the responsibility lay. While line managers and employees bear the final responsibility in adhering to the code, staff departments can play an important role in stimulating, monitoring and controlling adherence to the code.

TRANSLATION INTO PRACTICE . . .

1. What do you regard as the most important functions of your (potential) code (internally: orientating, clarifying, guiding, stimulating, initiating or corrective; and externally: distinguishing, legitimating or corrective)?

2. If your organisation already has a code, is justice being done to these functions?

3. Which metaphor for a code in your view expresses the function and meaning of the (potential) code?

4. If you were to ask your colleagues and employees to choose an object that represents the code, what would they put on the table?

5. What meaning could the code have for the various management disciplines within your organisation?

6. In what way can support staff departments play a role in the development and embedding of the code in your organisation?

5

The excellent code

A great variety of business codes exist in terms of scope, depth, wording and design. What does this mean? Is this a positive or rather negative observation? On the one hand, it is certainly positive. Apparently many companies make the effort to develop their own code. Instead of copying or downloading it from the internet, care is taken to develop a bespoke code.

On the other hand, it does not follow that a unique or special code is necessarily a good code. That would be too bold a statement. But, if there are so many different codes, is there still anything meaningful to say about the quality of a code? When is a code good? What is a good code?

This is not a question that can be answered readily. A code is partly also a question of taste. And there is no foolproof recipe or blueprint for a good code. It is nevertheless possible to distinguish a number of characteristics of a good code. In this chapter four important characteristics are discussed.

It is worthwhile to reflect on these characteristics before developing or renewing a code. What do the characteristics mean for our code? And what does this mean for the manner in which we develop the code? In addition, the characteristics are also important in understanding the current code, applying the code to your own conduct and for its embedding in the organisation. Awareness of the quality of the code also means that its strengths can be emphasised and its weaknesses can be compensated for or neutralised.

Four qualities of a good code

A good code has four qualities. A good code is (1) comprehensive, (2) morally justifiable, (3) authentic and (4) manageable.

FIGURE 5.1 Four qualities of a good code

Comprehensive

First it is important that the code encompasses all the company particularly stands for, that it addresses the issues the organisation is expected to respond to and that it gives guidance on the fundamental dilemmas that managers and employees confront.

A chemical company that fails to address environmental issues is missing the point entirely. A bank that ignores the issue of insider trading displays a gap in the content of the code. And a government institution that fails to attend to the acceptance of gifts by officials is overlooking a very important responsibility.

To ensure that the code covers the topics it should, it is important to explore the issues relevant to the organisation. What are the expectations of stakeholders? What issues are at play in the media, politics and society? Which dilemmas are managers and employees confronted with? And which issues do other organisations in the industry face?

The objective is not to include everything that can conceivably be addressed in the code. The idea is not that the more topics covered the better the code. Unfortunately, the latter tends to be the case in practice, especially for investment funds and scientific studies that seek to determine the quality of a code. The higher the number of topics covered in the code the higher the company scores. The art of writing, however, lies in deleting. Similarly, the art of developing a good code lies in naming the topics that are truly relevant to the organisation: those that are truly at stake and those that are sensible to include.

Sometimes issues are so self-evident that they need not even be included in a code. Not addressing something in a code does not imply that it is acceptable. The fact, for example, that there are few codes that prohibit employees from killing each other is not to say that the code is incomplete or that murdering colleagues is permitted. For something to be included in a code it should not only be an issue, but the code should also help to clarify situations that are unclear. Murder is clearly morally reprehensible, as is, exceptions aside, going to work in the nude or sending a family member as replacement in the event of illness. If all self-evident issues were to be included, the code would quickly grow into thousands of pages.

Comprehensive does not mean that all layers in the code pyramid should necessarily be found in the code. Generally, however, it is true that the more layers a code contains the better. Each layer has its own function and is of importance to the conduct of managers and employees. Most important is that when a particular type of code is chosen by a company the accompanying topics are comprehensive. An organisation that opts for a stakeholder statute and describes its responsibilities towards a range of external parties, but not towards its own staff displays a serious weakness and will evoke criticism (especially from the party that has to give content to the responsibilities towards external parties: namely, employees).

Thus if you want to examine the completeness of your code, it is important to establish what the relevant issues are and to what extent they are integrated into the code. Often it is better to make a list of relevant issues before examining the code rather than first reading the code and then checking whether any issues have been overlooked. The latter approach often curbs creativity and spontaneity and restricts one to the framework of the code. To put it to the test: does your code say anything about current issues such as the remuneration of management, supply chain responsibility, combating terrorism, sustainable development and stakeholder dialogue?

Morally justifiable

A second important requirement is that the company takes a morally justifiable position with respect to the issues the code addresses. In other words: that it is defensible, that it can withstand moral scrutiny and that general consensus can be reached on it. In particular, when the organisation itself refers to the code as an 'ethical code', it is important that the code is indeed ethical.

The fact that a topic is discussed does not say anything about its substance. It is not sufficient for a chemical company to address the environment in its code; the actual content should also be defensible. Obviously a phrase such as 'we try to maximise our negative impact on the natural environment' will be rejected outright. Similarly a code of a bank with the heading 'the customer always comes first' will be frowned on if it also assures criminal organisations that the bank would be pleased to assist them in money-laundering. And the government that encourages its officials to solicit gifts and entertainment from tendering parties is on a path that would not withstand moral scrutiny.

The question is therefore: when is a code morally legitimate? There are three criteria that apply. First, at a minimum, the code must be consistent with the laws and regulations of the countries in which the company operates. A code that undermines the prevailing rules and regulations will be morally unacceptable unless it can be demonstrated that the relevant laws and regulations are themselves morally unacceptable. Second, it is desirable that the code is in line with the generally accepted codes for businesses of national and international institutions, industry organisations and sectors. It is also desirable that the code is in line with the code of comparable companies. Is the company a front-runner, is it a leader or is it lagging behind? Third, there is the question of the extent to which the code reflects the expectations of stakeholders. Does it express what is important to them, does it address their needs and does it enhance their appreciation of the company?

The latter does not imply that everyone has to agree with the code. If that were the case, the code is likely to be a very drab and dreary document. If one is to avoid stepping on anyone's toes, one will end up saying very little. The aim should rather be that the code can in all reasonableness rely on acknowledgement and agreement. A code is good when it can rely on this sort of agreement. A code is excellent when it goes even further (Fig. 5.2). By setting new and progressive standards that are challenging, proactive and that inspire other organisations to follow, it may even yield applause and praise.

To be both accountable and responsible, the code has to be clearly written. Some codes excel at using woolly language and the reader would need to be a philosopher. Others excel at legal jargon and the reader would need to be lawyer. In both cases the question is whether it is helpful to its users. If ten readers of the same sentence each have different interpretations of the text, something is amiss. Sometimes companies acknowledge this problem and have the code simplified by a professional writer to make it clear to the general reader. Although there is nothing wrong with this, some companies have realised after distributing the code that the meaning of carefully constructed sentences had been altered.

The quality of a code is often determined not by what it says but what it does *not* say. What is omitted can be indicative of blind spots in the organisation or of conscious choices. And what's been scrapped, especially at the last moment, indicates what has been discussed most and what the

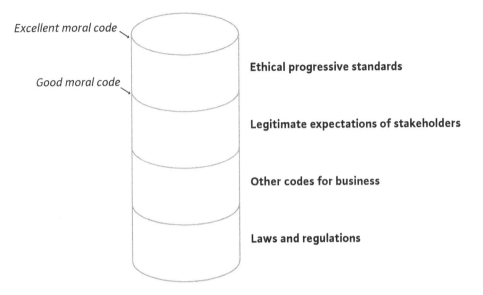

Excellent moral code

Ethical progressive standards

Good moral code

Legitimate expectations of stakeholders

Other codes for business

Laws and regulations

FIGURE 5.2 Four levels of morality

organisation would (not) dare commit to paper. Having made this remark, a board of directors I advised requested an overview of all modifications to the code's content to date. A surprisingly lively discussion followed. Whereas other boards of directors usually suggest deleting passages, this board came up with additions. Greater understanding was achieved of the proposed text and the complex considerations that informed important passages.

At a first reading one often only notices what is written in the code rather than what is omitted. It is only when one approaches it from the perspective of an incident, dilemma or issue that one truly understands what the code actually says—and does not say. One way of judging the quality of a code is therefore to examine what the code says with reference to a real dilemma at play in the organisation. In general, one can say that the more direction a code indicates for the specific dilemma, the better the quality of the code.

From the requirement that a code should be morally justifiable, it follows that it should also periodically be assessed on its relevance and modified where necessary. The more concrete a code, the more modification it will require. In view of rapidly changing societal issues and perspectives, along with internal company developments often also initiating change, it is implausible that a code can remain unchanged for decades. For example, recently updated codes pay more attention to climate change, corporate governance and transparency.

Authentic

Being complete and morally justifiable still does not make a code good. Even a model code can be entirely devoid of character. Such a code can very possibly be a literal replica of another business code. These 'copy–paste codes' do exist: only the name of the company is changed and, with luck, also the introduction. For quite a while, the Credo of Johnson & Johnson and the Shell Business Principles served as a point of departure for many companies in the development of their code. The Credo of Johnson & Johnson, which dates back to 1943, consists of one page describing the mission of the organisation and is structured around the four most important stakeholder groups (where consumers are named first and shareholders last). The Shell General Business Principles consists of eight principles, each of which is briefly elaborated on. A great risk of adopting another code as a point of departure is that one often does not make much progress from there. One quickly becomes entangled in the structure of such a code and its text with the result that only marginal adjustments are made.

With the rise of the internet it has become even easier to create a code by copying and pasting. Type in an issue with the second word 'code' and you'll come up with a multitude of quotes from codes. There are also websites where the codes of a diverse range of companies can be found. It might have become easier to create a code but it has also become easier to establish how original a code is (not). You can just type in one passage to see whether it can be found back in another code. Companies that adopt entire sections from other codes are easily exposed. And so was the compliance officer who had produced a code on request from the board.

The board was so impressed with the proposed text that it was adopted without any changes. A few weeks after the code had been disseminated the chairperson of the board met up with a very surprised manager. After some questioning it transpired that the code showed great similarities to that of his former employer. On closer examination it turned out that the compliance officer had 'borrowed' many passages of the other company's code somewhat too freely.

For the reasons discussed above it is therefore important that a code is authentic. That it's suited to the organisation. That it exudes the spirit of the organisation. That it doesn't only say something, but that what it says is significant, substantial. There is therefore no 'one-size-fits-all' code. The question, however, is, what is it that makes the code unique?

A test for the authenticity of the code is to present three anonymous codes to a group and to have them guess which belongs to your organisation. As an organisation you have a problem if your code is not selected more often than is statistically likely. The problem is even greater if people think that your code is that of a company in a wholly different industry or that they think that the code is for a multinational while you have fewer than 100 people employed.

An authentic code is appealing, attractive, alluring. It stipulates not only what *should not* be done, but also what *should* be done. Some codes excel in the repeated use of the word 'not'. The 'not' factor refers to the number of times the word 'not' or similar words such as 'no' or 'never' occurs in the code divided by the total number of words in the code. There are codes that score higher than 5%. One in twenty words is negative. No wonder, then, that the reader experiences the code as pedantic, restrictive and threatening.

A code is also authentic when it is whole, in the sense of an integrated whole. That it is not an ad hoc amalgamation of divergent elements, but that it flows, is harmonious and balanced. Companies often find this challenging. Knowing what you want to say differs from having a well-worked-out narrative with a logical structure. Of course, the code need not read as a novel but it must capture the reader's attention and invite them to read the entire text at least once.

Manageable

With the three characteristics above we're not quite there yet. A code can include all relevant issues, address them in an authentic and morally justifiable manner, but be so ambitious as to render it unrealistic. A fourth important characteristic of a good code is therefore that it is manageable, feasible, practicable.

Some codes move from one superlative to the next. Even if this has a heart-warming effect, it alienates if it amounts to empty promises. Checking its manageability entails examining what is, with good will and concerted effort, practically achievable over a period of three to five years. There will always be tension between what the code prescribes and current practice. In a certain sense that is also good. The code then becomes an instrument by means of which to improve current practices, to go one step further. If people have the impression that a substantial part of the code can never be realised, it can quickly be perceived as a document devoid of any content, mere words and mere window-dressing.

In addition to the tension between the code and current practice the question also arises as to what extent the code itself contains tensions. Does the code contradict itself or is it consistent as a whole? Does the code make conflicting demands thereby rendering it unrealisable? A code soon becomes contradictory if it speaks of maximising profits on the one hand and lifetime employment on the other. Or if it claims that the customer always comes first while at the same time adopting restrictive rules on accepting and processing new clients.

Understanding the code well implies being aware of the dilemmas contained in the code. A code is never free of dilemmas. Tensions will remain, which are also necessary to explore the limits of the code—in the positive sense of the term. For this reason companies sometimes provide guidelines to assist employees in dealing with dilemmas created by the code or dilemmas that are not addressed in the code.

If a code is to be manageable, it also has to be accessible in the sense of being readable, structured and easy to consult. It is also advisable for the code to be available in local languages. I still encounter companies in which, despite the fact that a substantial proportion of employees are not native English speakers, the code is available only in English. In contrast to this, companies such as Texas Instruments and Johnson & Johnson have their code published in 11 and 36 languages, respectively.

As summarised in Table 5.1, a good code meets at least four reasonable requirements. An excellent code is also morally progressive.

Qualities	Elements
Comprehensive	<ul><li>Relevant and current issues</li><li>Meaningful (most important issues)</li><li>Correct layers of the code pyramid</li></ul>
Morally justifiable	<ul><li>Legally watertight</li><li>Compatible with other codes</li><li>Defensible towards stakeholders (ethically sustainable)</li></ul>
Authentic	<ul><li>Striking and appealing (motivating)</li><li>Tailor-made and unique</li><li>Coherent</li><li>Fluent (flow)</li></ul>
Manageable	<ul><li>Readable and accessible</li><li>Well structured and clear</li><li>Internally consistent</li><li>Realisable in practice (realistic)</li></ul>

TABLE 5.1 Checklist for the quality of a code

Four issues in code development

Meeting the above-mentioned requirements is undoubtedly easier said than done. Developing a code involves making a number of choices. There are four questions companies struggle with in the development and introduction of a code which I discuss here. The way in which these issues are engaged with determines not only the direction of the code, but also its embedding.

Top-down and/or bottom-up?

The first question concerns who is to be involved in the development of the code and how intensively: only top management, a selection of employees, a committee or everyone? And external parties as well? Some companies opt for a quick approach involving as few as possible. The result is immediate and saves a lot of discussion and debate. Perhaps it is also a way for a company that is under pressure to develop a code in a short space of time and to embark on it energetically. The danger in this approach is, however, that the code may not receive support from those who have to adhere to it. Moreover, the question is also whether the developers are aware of the concrete problems and potential solutions that already exist within the organisation. However, the more people involved in the development of a code, the more time-consuming it is and the greater the potential that it could lead to endless discussions with an unsatisfactory outcome for all.

Values and/or rules?

A recurring question in the development of a code is the relationship between values and rules. Clear and distinct rules promote clarity and consistency. This is especially important if significant interests such as health and safety are at stake, or if one intends to link sanctions with zero tolerance of violations of the code.

Relying only on rules has certain significant disadvantages. First, rules are never conclusive. Not all actions can be captured in rules. There is always a grey area. An excess of rules has a debilitating or paralysing effect. Moreover, rules often lag behind developments. Creating rules for all possible scenarios and exceptions can rapidly expand a code. As one entrepreneur formulated it: 'The more rules you make, the more loopholes and the more ifs and buts you create.' In addition, the appeal of rules to individual responsibility is weak. Too many rules prevent employees from speaking out, promote uncertainty and conformism, create suspicion and therefore have a negative effect.

The advantage of values is that they have a more open character, appeal to individual insight, initiative and responsibility, and therefore have a more stimulating effect.

Diversity or unity?

Another pressing issue is the choice between unity and diversity. To what extent should the code lead to everyone having the same opinion? And what freedom do managers and employees retain?

On the one hand, the image the outside world has of an organisation should be coherent and consistent. For example, in cases of money-laundering one branch of a bank should follow the same procedure as another. It would also be unacceptable if one employee of a recruitment agency adheres to policies on discrimination while another ignores them.

On the other hand, individual subsidiaries will desire a degree of independence, especially if they are spread throughout the world. The desire for a certain level of uniformity should leave room for individual understanding and insight. Too much emphasis on unity promotes conformism, undermines decentralised and individual responsibility and leads to rigidity and evasive behaviour. Moreover, the more a company grows internationally, the more it is confronted with different local circumstances. A gift of $50 has a different value in developed countries from that in developing countries.

Ambitions or practice?

A fourth issue that is often encountered concerns the consideration of ambitions on the one hand and actual practice on the other. Should the code take up generally accepted standards and expectations or should it focus on changing them? Formulated differently: should a code be realistic or ambitious?

A code seldom signifies a radical break with the past, but rather builds on that which is already in place. The code articulates, emphasises and strengthens existing views that, albeit implicit and sometimes underdeveloped, already exist within the organisation. It can elicit reactions such as: 'But we already know that. What is written in the code is nothing new!' This is—to some extent—the greatest compliment one can get for a code.

At the same time a code is more than the sum or common denominator of existing practice. Where generally accepted standards and expectations are inconsistent or undesirable, they need to be refined or modified. The code can therefore also be ambitious and promote change. It is important, however, that the code does not become a collection of hollow phrases disconnected from reality.

TRANSLATION INTO PRACTICE . . .

1. To what extent do you endorse the four characteristics and qualities of a good code as discussed in this chapter?

2. Are there, in your opinion, other characteristics as well? If so, which? And how do they relate to those discussed in this chapter?

3. To what extent does the (desired) code of your organisation meet each of these characteristics? In other words, what are the strengths and weaknesses of the code?

4. To what extent can your (desired) code be described as excellent? In other words, to what extent is the code morally progressive?

5. To what extent do or did the four issues of the development of a code as discussed in this chapter play a role within your organisation? And how did or will you resolve it?

6

The nightmare code

A company presented its new code and received overwhelming media attention. From then on the company would live by its unique principles. Neither cost nor effort was spared in its presentation. Several communication activities involving employees and external stakeholders took place. The board gave interviews emphasising the uniqueness of the code and the vigour and conviction with which they intended to introduce it. Up until that moment everything was going well. A few weeks later the police raided the company. The board was suspected of large-scale fraud: for years not only the Inland Revenue, but also customers and competitors had been cheated of millions. Through all sorts of ingenious constructions the company had also managed to restrict competition: for example, through price fixing with the bigger players in the industry. The reprehensible practices of the company were in sharp contrast with the code: 'We strive for openness and transparency . . .', 'We support fair competition . . .' and 'Employees should enter financial transactions accurately and honestly in keeping with the prevailing accounting principles.' It comes as little surprise that the company, code and all, was subsequently mercilessly pilloried. In the eyes of employees, management had fallen flat on its face. No wonder the code, after its stormy introduction, was, in the words of one of the directors, 'shelved very quickly'.

The introduction of a business code can be a nightmare. The code can turn out to be a mockery. It can encounter significant resistance and create great upheaval. A code can be granted only a short life and turn out to be a one-day wonder, nothing more than an empty shell or window-dressing. The code disappears to the bottom of the desk drawer or the bin. Just as in the example, the code can boomerang back and inflict damage on the credibility and image of the organisation. The code haunts the organisation and the board sighs: 'If only we had never started on this.'

In this chapter a variety of common mistakes will be discussed. Examples are taken from the launches of codes that did not proceed smoothly. After this cold shower, we will examine how to make a success of a code in the chapters that follow.

Blunders

There's a lot that can go wrong in the introduction of a code. In this section we discuss some of the worst-case scenarios that occur more regularly than one would perhaps expect. The companies discussed also thought that they had everything under control when they launched their code.

- **The visible corrections.** The team that had developed the code sent the final draft electronically to all employees. By means of the revision feature employees were able to examine which changes had been made to previous texts. To make matters worse, comments were included such as: 'Level six or lower won't understand this' and 'Won't this create problems in our pending court case?'

- **By return mail.** At one company the code was sent to employees accompanied by a request to confirm receipt by signing an attached letter and returning it to the board. Instead of sending the letter, many employees sent back the code itself with comments like 'Recipient unknown', 'Do not do unto others what you do not want others to do you', 'Fools rush in where angels fear to tread', 'Point a finger at someone and soon you'll find three pointing at yourself'. Some employees used the code to make paper aeroplanes which they demonstratively threw out of the windows of the top floor. In one department the code was torn up—after removing the staples—and put in the toilets to serve as toilet paper

- **The eager procurer.** One company sent its new code to its suppliers including a letter that informed them that the code would be incorporated into all master contracts. The letter also stated that the company trusted that suppliers would not pressurise company employees into acting in a manner that conflicts with the code. A day later the director of procurement quite blatantly requested one of the biggest suppliers to deliver a few pleasant surprises to his home address before the new contract negotiations could start. This was in full violation of the code, which, when employees heard about it, undermined the whole code and its compliance programme

- **A thin layer of varnish.** A week after the company announced its recently completed code during its annual shareholders' meeting, a national supervisory body revealed that the company had been committing serious environmental fraud for years. According to the supervisory body the fraud had been going on up to the day the code was published. The code contained an entire chapter on how seriously the company took its environmental responsibilities. To make matters worse, it later transpired that tax fraud and purchasing fraud was also standard practice in the company

- **The wayward successor.** Under the enthusiastic leadership of the CEO a code was established. Much time and effort was invested in it both internally and externally. Soon after his successor replaced him the code was declared a superfluous luxury. The stakeholders with whom the code was discussed in great detail were astonished and regarded it as a typical example of the inconsistency and unreliability of the board of that company

- **The uninformed board member.** In a radio interview an executive claimed that his company had no code while the company had introduced a code with much fanfare less than six months earlier. The reporter was better informed and exposed the interviewee to be at least six months behind developments in his company. The reporter could not resist the temptation to ask the executive whether he was sure there were not perhaps other areas in his company of which he was just as unaware

- **The journalist at the gates.** Two years after the introduction of a code for which the company held dozens of presentations to outsiders, a newspaper journalist questioned employees leaving the premises to discover what had become of the code. The journalist expected a range of positive reactions. To his surprise more than half of the employees claimed never to have seen the code. You can just imagine the headlines

The above, real, examples are anecdotal. Hopefully they demonstrate how a code can go wrong and make an organisation look foolish, consequently leading to even more problems instead of resolving any.

A false start

A code that flops often goes wrong very quickly—often in the way it is initially launched or presented. A few destructive comments from management that frequently occur and which should be avoided are:

- **'The order to implement the code has come from the top.'** There is no greater show of incompetence of middle and lower management if they present themselves as the mouthpiece or messenger of the board. If management is not intrinsically motivated to implement the code, it should not come as a surprise if employees are not intrinsically motivated to comply with it

- **'Every respectable company has a code!'** This statement as such is correct, but if it is presented as the main reason for hav-

ing a code it comes across as being reactive and insufficiently
driven from within

- **'Regard the code as an ambition not as the bottom line.'** Even
if it can be true, such a comment does invite too broad an interpretation. With one fell swoop such a remark does away with
any pressure to comply

- **'The code is important. But profits are more important!'** This
comment also marginalises the code. If profitability is always
paramount, then the code will always be sidelined. In addition,
such a remark suggests that compliance and long-term profitability are by definition incompatible

- **'The code is crystal clear.'** No matter how a good a code is, it
always requires translation from paper to practice where users
must seek to understand and interpret it accurately. By suggesting that the code is completely clear, employees who are unsure
about its meaning will be reluctant to ask questions. 'If you have
questions there must be something wrong with your reading
ability' is the reasoning, they might fear

- **'You are sensible enough to determine yourself what the code
means for your conduct.'** This is only a half-truth. The power of
a code lies precisely in the discussions one has with colleagues
and examining the meaning of the code for individual and collective conduct

- **'The code is intended to make matters discussable!'** Even
though one of the functions of a code is to bring dilemmas to the
fore for discussion, such statements are often made by managers who have little interest in being guided by the content of
the code. Under the adage 'as long we are open about things' and
'as long as it's been discussed' all other ethical considerations
are swept under the carpet and every decision is right

- **'The code is about doing!'** A code does indeed turn on compliance. But there is more to it than simply abiding by it. The organisation should also make an effort if employees are to uphold it.

Moreover, complying with the code does not amount to following it blindly. Adhering to a code involves skill and intelligence

- ⬡ **'If you do not comply with the code you will be fired!'** Such a statement testifies to a strong commitment, but perhaps too strong a commitment. If the code also articulates the company's ambitions, full compliance (in the short term) will be impossible. Such a statement instils fear among employees with the result that dilemmas and discrepancies may not be discussed but instead covered up, remaining invisible to the higher ranks

Such an unfortunate beginning can contribute to negative reactions among employees. As a result they can perceive a code as:

- ⬡ **Senseless.** Employees regard the code as a vacuous document consisting of hollow phrases and false ambitions that have no credibility: 'This is the umpteenth paper tiger' and 'This is the same old story phrased differently'

- ⬡ **Restrictive.** Employees regard the code as merely articulating restrictions, failing to indicate what may and should be done in particular circumstances. 'This code is a millstone' and 'The code prevents me from carrying out my work'

- ⬡ **Obstructive.** Employees see the code as conflicting with what is economically and financially viable. The code is seen as too politically correct: 'Will we still be able to generate a profit?', 'Should this not also apply to our competitors?' and 'What is the point of having a code if we will go under?'

- ⬡ **Pedantic.** Employees regard the code as pedantic, as the ten commandments of the organisation, as something almost spiritual and religious: 'I do it my way and that's it', 'Isn't the code just common sense?' and 'If they think they can replace my conscience with a code and brainwash me, I'm resigning'

- ⬡ **Threatening.** Employees view the code as a vote of no confidence, a stick rather than a carrot and a rope around the neck. 'The code is like Russian roulette: it is a matter of chance who gets caught first and sacked'

- **Only intended for others.** Employees see the code as a means to help bring employees with dubious intentions on the right path. 'The code is intended only for the 5% that are predisposed to committing violations. The code is not relevant at all for the remaining 95%.' And 'why should the good guys always suffer because of the bad guys?'

- **Disconnected.** Employees see the code as far removed from daily practice and a policy document of importance only to the top of the organisation. 'The code is for the boardroom not for us in the back office' and 'The code only concerns major, strategic issues while my everyday concerns are of a very different, much more practical nature'

- **Window-dressing.** Employees see the code as smooth talk intended to pacify annoying outsiders. 'The code has just one purpose: to keep our stakeholders naive, stupid and ignorant' and 'Do you really think they believe it and don't see through it?'

- **A means to shirk responsibility.** Employees see the code as a means to shirk responsibility: it rids them of their conscience and allows them to hide behind the code. 'That which is not covered in the code is permitted' and 'I only have to do what the code prescribes'

- **A hype.** Employees see the code as a whim that will blow over soon. 'Tomorrow management will come up with a new toy' and 'Just ignore it, it will blow over soon enough'

- **Idealistic.** Employees see the code as high-flown and overly ambitious, so idealistic that it loses all appeal. 'One would swear we had become a charity' and 'Is this code not a nail in our coffin?'

Painful consequences

If the above views are not corrected swiftly, a very undesirable state of affairs can follow. A few consequences from practice are listed below:

- **No addressee.** The code does not appeal to employees with the result that it goes over their heads and remains suspended in a vacuum

- **No energy.** The code does not generate the energy required to work towards realising it. The code leaves employees cold; it fails to stimulate

- **Atmosphere of mistrust.** The code is counterproductive in that employees regard it as a motion of no confidence. 'If they want to teach me a lesson, I will teach them.' Instead of having a constructive effect it is destructive

- **Undermining behaviour.** As a result of the lack of support, employees try to avoid and undermine the code. Sometimes employees even see it as a challenge or game to do exactly what the code prohibits. 'We shall see who gets the worst of it' according to one recalcitrant employee against whom investigations of fraud were later launched

- **Stretching the boundaries.** Employees are stimulated to interpret the code creatively while remaining within its limits by balancing on the edge or they are challenged to keep pushing the limits or actively seeking out loopholes

- **Silence.** The code silences employees. 'If you have any questions, please read the code. And if you still have questions, you can't read.' The code has a choking effect. It's the last word. The end to all discussion

- **Bureaucratic behaviour.** The code robs employees of their sense of personal responsibility. Employees look up what they must do in a given situation. They do what's written there. If the code does not cover the particular situation they're free to do as they like

- **Negative communication towards the outside world.** Employees experience the code as such a farce that they spout their dissatisfaction to the outside world. It becomes grounds for external whistle-blowing. Deviations from the code can appear in the form of letters to newspapers

- **Sharp criticism.** With the code in hand employees find fault with everything and challenge colleagues to remove the mote from their eyes without considering the beam in their own

- **Minimalism.** The less attention the code is paid the better. This is the attitude of employees who regard the code as only relevant to violations and deviant behaviour

As we've seen in this chapter a code can be a real nightmare. A diverse range of blunders and mishaps can occur. A false start with grievous consequences for the organisation is not inconceivable. Also on a personal level miscommunication of the code can have annoying consequences. Engraved in my memory in this regard is the director who like all other directors in the company was asked to roll out the code in his division. Owing to all sorts of other priorities and urgent matters he did not manage to introduce the code well. To be sure, he did disseminate the code among employees, but any real discussion failed to take place.

Three years later it transpired that a team in his division had been involved in price fixing with competitors resulting in the conclusion of a number of very lucrative contracts. A competitor who did not form part of the group and whose business suffered as a result, decided to take legal action. An important lead was the organisation's code which explicitly prohibited price fixing. It also stated that management had the responsibility to create a work environment that promoted compliance with the code and detecting violations in time. This turned out not to be the case. The offenders denied ever having received the code. They also maintained in court that the pressure in the organisation was such that they were forced to partake in price fixing.

When the director was subsequently asked to explain himself he could not prove that his employees had in fact received the code. And since there was no evidence of any other activity to introduce the code the director's position was even more precarious. This became all the more apparent when the judge found that the other directors in the company had put great effort into introducing the code in their division. When it was found that the director employed a very aggressive remuneration system it was clear to the judge that the director had been negligent and was an accessory to the violations. The company was given a fine. And with the code in hand, the director was sacked while his employees were given a reprimand.

TRANSLATION INTO PRACTICE . . .

1. How do you judge the code of your organisation? And what was your first reaction when you received the code?

2. How did or would outsiders, managers and employees judge the code in the latest or its first introduction? And what was their reaction or what will it be when the code is announced or received?

3. What should you absolutely refrain from saying or doing and what should you absolutely say or do in order to avoid negative reactions during the launch of the code?

4. To what extent should you give people the opportunity to voice their doubts and misgivings regarding the code?

5. What are the potential nightmares surrounding the introduction and implementation of the code in your organisation?

6. What are the minimum precautions that should be taken to prevent or rectify these nightmares?

7

The code star

In the previous chapter we saw how the introduction of a code can go awry. The question this raises is how to go about introducing a code successfully. In this chapter, seven conditions are discussed that should be present in an organisation if the code is to be complied with. The chapter concludes with an overview of red flags: situations in which these seven conditions are either absent or too strongly present. Just as advocated in the virtue ethic of the Greek philosopher Aristotle, success is about reaching the mean of each of these seven conditions.

Seven conditions for a living code

I have conducted extensive scientific research into the causes of non-compliance with codes by managers and employees. In the examination of the conduct of managers and employees the role of the organisation received special attention. What impact do the culture, policy and strategy of the organisation have on their conduct? How does the organisation influence people? How does the organisation stimulate managers and employees to obey or disobey the code? In addition to examining the literature, I have collected 150 diverging incidents and investigated their causes. A number of statistical analyses ultimately yielded seven conditions.

These conditions, as depicted in Figure 7.1 as a star and in Figure 1.1 as the heart of the steering wheel in the code cockpit, are to be regarded as the preconditions for a living code. Embedding the code is also grounded in these seven conditions. They anchor the living code within an organisation. An organisation in which these conditions are present creates an optimal environment for managers and employees to comply with the code. If these conditions are absent or are too strongly present the organisation creates an environment in which non-compliance of managers and employees is inevitable.

The seven conditions can also be regarded as capabilities or capacities. The first two conditions concern the self-regulatory capacity of an organisation; the following two concern the self-supporting capacity of the

FIGURE 7.1 Seven conditions for a living code

organisation; and the last three conditions together concern the self-cleansing capacity of the organisation.

Clarity

First, it is of importance that managers and employees have clarity on what is expected of them. That a code is clear does not necessarily mean that its meaning is clear to employees and managers. Despite the existence of a clear business code, individuals could be unaware of it, or they could be aware of it but interpret it in a different or even contradictory manner. The first condition therefore pertains to the knowledge of managers and employees: do they understand what the code entails?

Much reprehensible behaviour within organisations occurs not due to the lack of a code, since often there is one, but because perpetrators are not aware of the code. Awareness is not only about being aware of the existence of a code but, crucially, being familiar with its content and understanding what it means for one's own conduct. It is therefore not a matter of whether the code itself is clear, but whether it is clear to those who have to abide by it. It thus concerns their experience, perception, interpretation and judgement of the content of the code. What may appear clear on paper may well raise many questions to people in practice.

The question for each organisation with a code is: how clearly do managers and employees understand what is expected of them? How clear are the mission, values, responsibilities, norms and values? Do they know how to engage with sideline activities, gifts and organisational resources? And can they explain why these norms are in place and what their relation is to the mission, values and responsibilities of the organisation?

Good role-modelling

Setting a good example will generate good conduct among subordinates. But bad examples will generate bad conduct. Deviant behaviour of employees is often preceded by similar behaviour from leadership.

Employees who see their boss declaring fictitious costs with a casual attitude towards rules will soon think: 'If my boss can, why shouldn't I?'

Or employees who know that their boss has accepted special private treatment by suppliers will be more inclined to avail themselves of such practices. And employees who see their superiors cheating clients will be more inclined to treat their own clients in the same manner.

Management is an important source in determining which code truly applies. Does the explicit code really count or is there another, implicit code at work? People read this from the behaviour of their manager. The manager is the walking and talking business code! Through their conduct management can reinforce or undermine the code.

The questions for each organisation with a code are therefore: To what extent does management, from top to bottom, set a good example? What importance do they attribute to the code? Are they leaders in complying with the code? And is their exemplary behaviour also seen and appreciated as such? Thus, it's not only about what management does, but also how it is perceived by others.

Commitment

The code may be clear for managers and employees and leadership may set a good example, but the code can still be violated. Violations of the code can be caused by a lack of motivation and loyalty, or even resistance, anger and vengeance. In my research I came across incidents where employees blame their organisation because they feel disrespected and slighted. For example, an employee diverted large amounts of money to his private account because he did not receive the raise he had been promised and which, in his mind, he thoroughly earned. Or the employee who had been suffering so much under the intimidating style of his manager that he decided to take revenge by sabotaging the production system. Both employees decided to take the law into their own hands to settle the score.

The third condition for a living code is, therefore, to ensure that motivation, intent and effort among managers and employees to comply with the code are nurtured. That is, that managers and employees identify with the organisation and the code in the correct manner; that they feel a sense of commitment.

The question for each organisation with a code is therefore: Are employees committed to the organisation and its mission and objectives? Do they identify with the code of the organisation? Are they committed to their work? In other words: To what extent does the organisation inspire management and employees to internalise the code? Or do managers and employees see the code as a threat, restriction or limitation to their professionalism and integrity?

Feasibility

In addition to awareness and commitment it is important that managers and employees are capable of upholding the code. Are they sufficiently equipped to realise the code? The fourth condition for a living code concerns the question of the extent to which the organisation enables managers and employees to comply with the code.

Violations of the code often occur as a result of unrealistic targets or a lack of means available for employees to carry out their tasks in a responsible manner. Over-optimistic targets can force people into taking short cuts. Annual double-digit growth targets are bound to push people to breaking point. The sales person whose targets are raised each quarter could easily find him- or herself in a situation where guile and deceit appear the only solution.

For each organisation the following questions need to be answered. To what extent do current targets place pressure on managers and employees? To what extent do they believe that these ends justify the means? Do they have sufficient resources at their disposal? Is the desired conduct as stipulated by the code realisable in practice? Which developments and parties within and outside the organisation put a strain on compliance with the code? And how long are managers and employees resistant to the pressure and at what point do they break? Do they let themselves go or bite off more than they can chew?

Transparency

The first four conditions are largely about stimulating compliance and preventing violations of the code. The fifth condition concerns the degree to which violations can be detected. It therefore concerns the transparency of the organisation and business conduct.

The greater the transparency, the more visible violations and the more readily an organisation can intervene. There is a multitude of examples of secret violations that have allowed the 'tumour' to grow: employees increasingly violating the code without management discovering it; middle management keeping reprehensible behaviour out of the board's field of vision; the board frequently violating the code while employees, supervisors and outsiders are none the wiser.

Transparency also has a preventive function. Sunlight is the best disinfectant. Scientific research has shown that the lower the chance of detection the higher the number of violations. The perceived likelihood of being caught does influence behaviour. Transparency casts its shadow ahead.

For every organisation with a code the following questions arise: To what extent are violations visible and are 'checks' adequately carried out? To what extent are the effects of behaviour visible to managers and employees? What does the top know about the rest of the organisation? What don't they know and what should they know? How visible is the conduct of the top? And is there adequate supervision on that?

Discussability

It is also important that the code is and remains a topic of discussion. Where there is a taboo about talking about the code, a culture of different and even conflicting interpretations of the content of the code may quickly develop. Staff then may also feel unable to share their dilemmas and consequently perceive a lack of support in bringing the code alive. Because a code can never be totally complete and always requires translation to practice, it is important that managers and employees are able to discuss it with each other. The sixth condition, discussability, reduces the chance of misinterpretation and broadens support from within the organisation for the decisions managers and employees take.

Additionally it is important that, when violations of the code are identified, offenders can and are indeed challenged. If this does not happen, a hush-hush policy quickly develops itself with the potential of growing into a serious problem for the organisation. Social control is an important condition for keeping a code alive.

For each organisation with a code there are questions such as: To what extent are dilemmas that are related to the code discussable? Can employees challenge each other and their manager on alleged violations of the code? Is criticism heeded? Or does the whistle-blower get the proverbial axe? And does everyone scratch each other's back?

Enforcement

Finally it is important that, when a breach of the code by a manager or employee has been ascertained, they are punished. There is nothing as deadly as a code that is introduced with great fanfare only to be followed by a manager who very visibly violates it and gets away scot-free. Failing to punish violations of the code implies that (a) the code does not apply to everyone; or (b) that it applies to no one!

The seventh condition for a living code thus concerns enforcing the code in the organisation. It is not only about punishing violations but also showing appreciation for adherence to the code. Appreciation does not necessarily have to be accompanied by financial reward. In this regard one could say that adherence to the code should be standard practice and that a financial reward would create the impression that it is an extraordinary achievement. What's most important is that managers and employees feel that compliance is appreciated, that it is acknowledged and that one receives credit for it.

Relevant questions for each organisation with a code are: To what extent are transgressions of the code punished? To what extent is punishment meted out fairly? Is compliance with the code appreciated and how is this demonstrated?

Red flags

These seven conditions form the foundation for compliance with the code and they are present in every organisation with a living code. With these prerequisites in place managers and employees are clear on what is expected of them. Dilemmas are discussable and managers and employees are challenged on questionable behaviour. In such an organisation the code star sparkles and shines brightly.

If an employee still violates the code in such circumstances, the organisation and management are not to blame. It has after all done its utmost to prevent violations from occurring. That it still occurs is because of a rotten apple against which no organisation can be entirely resistant. A judge or supervisory authority will have to take this into consideration in determining the punishment imposed.

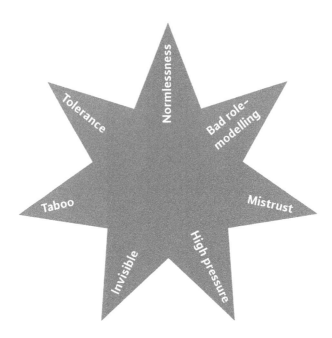

FIGURE 7.2 Red flags indicating the absence of the conditions for a living code

At the same time the absence of these conditions can be represented by red flags. The organisation finds itself on dangerous ground. This is the alarm phase where there is a lack of norms, bad role-modelling and distrust; where there is too much pressure to meet targets, invisibility, a taboo on discussing dilemmas and criticism, and violations are tolerated. Figure 7.2 depicts the seven red flags. An organisation that is characterised by the seven red flags is in fact asking for managers and employees to disobey the code. Transgressions are almost certain and it will be a matter of time if they not are already taking place. If an employee commits a violation, the organisation will be subjected to criticism and have a very hard time showing that it is blameless.

Another possibility can also occur. The seven conditions can be too prevalent. The organisation goes to such an extreme that there is too much of a good thing. As depicted in Figure 7.3, there is evidence of paternalism, pompousness and excessive exemplary behaviour of leaders,

FIGURE 7.3 Red flags indicating the excessive presence of the conditions for a living code

slave-like obedience of the code by managers and employees, extravagance and wastefulness of organisational means, information overload, interference and the relentless and ruthless enforcement of the code. Different instances of accounting fraud have revealed that the managers concerned became blind to their own behaviour. People identified with the organisation to such an extent that they lost their critical distance and could no longer accommodate other legitimate interests and viewpoints.

In sum, the art is to embed these seven conditions for a living code in a manner which strikes a happy medium—a balance between too little and too much embeddedness in the organisation.

TRANSLATION INTO PRACTICE . . .

1. To what degree are the seven conditions for a living code present in your organisation?

2. To what extent can the seven red flags signalling the absence of the seven conditions for a living code already be discerned in your organisation?

3. And to what extent can the seven red flags signalling the excessive presence of the conditions for a living code already be discerned in your organisation?

4. In what way do you think the correct balance between too much and too little of these seven conditions can be achieved?

5. What is the relationship between the seven conditions? Is there a specific order, connection and hierarchy?

6. To what extent have you internalised the seven conditions for a living code? Is the code clear to me? Do I set a good example? Do I fully endorse the code? Do I possess the capacity to realise the code? Am I transparent in my behaviour and do I know what I'm doing? Do I have any eye for my own dilemmas, do I make them discussable and can I be challenged on my behaviour? Do violations annoy me and am I constantly working on improving my compliance with the code?

8

Leadership, leadership and leadership again

We only made one mistake in the introduction of the code. The nature of the mistake, however, was such that it torpedoed the entire project. We invested so much energy in the development of the code. There were round-table discussions with employees, an inventory of existing dilemmas was made and a specially assigned committee presented the draft to us as the board. Our entire board of management discussed the code intensively and formalised it. What we did not adequately realise was that the work had only just begun. As a result of the intensive preparations we were somewhat 'code-worn'. We forgot the 20–80 rule: 20% inspiration and 80% perspiration. Or rather: 20% energy on the development of the code and 80% on introduction and implementation. We distributed the code among all managers and employees but erroneously assumed that the discussion and improvement programmes would take off by themselves. Unfortunately. Now, half a year later the code has sunk so far that we haven't made any progress at all.

According the director in the above quote a code is 20% inspiration and 80% perspiration. Even if this rule of thumb is not scientifically proven, its meaning is clear. Merely developing a code is not sufficient. Not by far. Embedding a code requires perseverance and substantial effort. A living code requires a powerful introduction and intensive maintenance. And to embed the code well, intelligence and insight are required.

The embedding of a code is therefore first and foremost a question of leadership. In this regard leadership cannot be emphasised enough. Leadership is not only about adhering to the code. Neither is it sufficient to demonstrate compliance. In that case leadership would be limited to the second condition for a living code: namely, good role-modelling behaviour. Leadership is about embedding the seven conditions as discussed in the previous chapter in such a manner that employees are fully stimulated to comply with the code.

In this chapter, leadership requirements are discussed in relation to each element of the code star. These guidelines are based on the experience of companies that have had greater or lesser success in embedding their code and on discussions about it with managers, employees and supporting staff such as compliance and ethics officers.

These guidelines are characterised by a process approach: a code is nothing; coding is everything. Embedding a code is largely about jointly thinking through its meaning, jointly articulating expectations and commitment, and jointly creating measures and activities to keep the code alive. The codification process unlocks the wealth embodied in a code.

Clarity: internalising the code

Leadership first requires that the code is internalised, both by yourself and by your employees. It concerns the following aspects.

Memorise the code

To adhere to the code, knowledge of its content is a prerequisite. Knowledge precedes compliance. Knowing what is written in the code therefore is an absolute must. This is often thought to be somewhat pedantic and that just the general thrust of the code is important. Too often, however, managers don't have the code to hand or cannot find the relevant passages quickly enough. It becomes all the more annoying when a manager makes statements that conflict with the code which others have to draw his or her attention to. Not to mention managers who unknowingly and unintentionally systematically violate the code and have to be made aware of this by their own employees. Skimming or paging through the code is not sufficient to let it sink in. Memorise the code. Know its content by heart; or, if the code is very long, know its main parts.

Work through practical examples to understand the code better

It is not only about what is written in the code. It is also about knowing what the code means, to understand its message, to grasp its implications. Understanding the code requires study. It is important to analyse the text of the code carefully and thoughtfully. A good leader will think through the essence of the meaning of each paragraph to acquire a feel for the language of the code. Countless and very fundamental discussions could have preceded each formulation. In this way, one company changed a phrase in the new version of its code from 'We would like to inform our stakeholders of important matters' to 'We would like to communicate important matters with our stakeholders'. One slight change, but for the company it signified the adoption of an entirely different world-view. From a rather arrogant attitude where the company determined what stakeholders were told to one that was much more respectful, where the company engaged stakeholders in dialogue because they may be aware of things that the company did not know.

A few exercises in better understanding the code are:

- Can I summarise the code? If a journalist were to ask about the content of the code would I be able to sketch the broad outlines? If not, write a summary for yourself

- Can I explain how the code relates to external codes that apply to the organisation and my work? If not, request a copy of the external codes and examine them

- Can I explain how the code is related to those of competitors and peers? If not, request a copy of their codes and compare them

- Can I explain how the code relates to internal sub-codes and other documents with rules for conduct? If not, study the relations and check whether you have a thorough overview of internal sub-codes

- Can I explain each line or even sentence with an example of what it does and does not mean? If not, look at the code and write down such examples

- What does the code refrain from addressing? Can I name three issues that are not included in the code? And can I indicate by each issue that is addressed in the code which norms and prescriptions are omitted? If not, take time to come up with examples or if necessary approach the developers of the code for assistance

Through thorough examination and reflection one will eventually be able to play, or juggle with the code, to grasp it thoroughly and know it by heart.

Devote time for employees' first encounter with the code

Introducing a code involves translating it so that it acquires concrete and appropriate meaning for employees; so that it is interpreted correctly by those who have to use it. For this reason it is critical to systematically think through the meaning and purpose of the code. In order for employees to truly absorb the meaning of the code, it is essential to set aside time for it. It is not sufficient to distribute the code and subsequently ask whether there are any questions. In particular, if the code contains clichés it will be regarded as old hat and not worthy of further attention. Even if the code does not contain anything new, it still does not imply that business conduct is consistent with the code.

Ensure that employees know the content of the code

Knowledge of the content is just as important for employees as it is for managers. Do not rest until you are sure that employees know its content. Do not only stimulate them to read the code, but question them on their knowledge of the code. Show that you expect them to know the code. By this, I don't mean that it is necessary to formally test employees on their knowledge of the code. Some companies do this. Employees are subjected to an exam where the correct quote must be selected by case or question. I know of a company where employees who failed the web-based test twice (lower than six out of ten questions) were obliged to undergo an in-depth interview with their supervisor. Failing three times resulted in a course and failing five times led to a change of function or dismissal. Dismissals incidentally never materialised given that the number of people who failed five times was so high that following this course would have been too great a drain on company resources!

Emphasise underlying values and responsibilities

In order for employees to understand the code, it is important to discuss the underlying responsibilities and values. What is the basis on which the code has been drawn up? What are the drivers of the code? What are the underlying considerations? Merely communicating the norms and rules has, as discussed in Chapter 5, diverse risks. If one wants to communicate the norms and rules it is advisable to start at the beginning; to discuss the higher levels of the code pyramid. In this way one learns to understand the norms and rules and place them in a broader context. By starting at the top of the pyramid and working one's way down, employees are exposed to the spirit of the norms and rules (the bottom layer) which promotes adherence to it. The degree to which people are receptive to the upper layers of the pyramid depends on their moral capacity. Some people simply want to know what they should do. General values and responsibilities are too vague for them and too difficult to apply to their own behaviour. Others, however, appreciate the greater narrative or even regard it as sufficient and are capable of translating it themselves.

Teach employees to translate the code into personal conduct

Each employee has to be able to translate the purpose and content of the code to their own situation. The code has to have consequences for their individual conduct. The code must have a personal message. Knowledge of the contents is pointless if it cannot be related to personal conduct. Questions in this regard include:

- What does the code truly mean for me?

- How should I translate the code in my daily practice?

- To what extent am I already fulfilling the code?

- Which aspect of my conduct should I change and in what sense?

- And, if so, how should I change my conduct?

Embedding a code is therefore an introspective process in which each person examines what the code means for their own conduct. At the same time it is also a joint process. A code also has implications for the way in which a group, division or team engages with each other and with others. For this reason it is important to jointly think through the meaning of the code and jointly determine what implications it has for collective conduct.

Make sure the code hurts

The code should not only be translated to one's personal work situation. To avoid the code being thought of as pompous and woolly, it must be made tangible and concrete. Indeed, it must touch employees within. A code that does not stir emotions misses its point. A code should appeal to people and they should also feel appealed to. A code should, especially in the first introduction, champion different behaviour. In that sense a code should also hurt: it should put a stop to lucrative activities that are no longer allowed. At the same time, it does not imply that a new code should be accompanied by a watershed, metamorphosis or revolution. Changes in behaviour can be found in small things, such as showing more appreciation for each other or enquiring after customers' expectations and experiences of the organisation.

Ask employees about their own code

The code formulates what the organisation expects of employees. Just as important a question is what employees expect of the organisation. A code can conflict with the personal beliefs of employees. For this reason it is important to ask employees about their own personal code and how it relates to the business code. Their answers will show what they believe and what the similarities and differences are between both codes. Such questions prevent the code from being viewed as one-way communication and also promote the idea that the code is a shared document about which dialogue takes place.

Point out the limitations of the code

It is wonderful when a manager praises, applauds and celebrates a code. Such enthusiasm could, however, create the impression that the code is a panacea for all problems. A huge risk in such situations is that the expectations of employees and external parties are raised to such levels that the limitations of the code are overlooked. Under such circumstances the code can only be a disappointment in terms of content, embedding and compliance. Communication of the added value of the code should therefore preferably be accompanied by an emphasis on its limitations: the code says a lot but also nothing without embedding and compliance.

Determine how flexible or rigid you want to be

The question that comes up during the introduction of each code is to what extent the code should be interpreted literally. Should the letter of the code be adhered to in every detail or should the code be seen as the expression of an ambition, an aspiration where there is room for flexibility, interpretation and tolerance of deviations? Is the code a minimum, the foundation and point of departure or is it the maximum, the ceiling and final destination? If an organisation does not have a clear vision on this, it could give rise to very divergent viewpoints and conduct of managers and employees.

Choose the right moment to introduce and communicate the code

With the first introduction in particular it is important to give employees sufficient time to think through and absorb the code. For this reason it is important that the code is not introduced at the busiest time of the year. As thinking through the code is mostly a joint process, it is likewise important to choose a time when most people are present. The company that decided to introduce its code during the summer holidays was misguided in two respects. Because the capacity of the teams was halved, the remaining employees were very busy keeping the company running with the result that discussion of the code was brief and inadequate. In addition, those returning to work found the code among a heap of other documents and felt overwhelmed that such a far-reaching document had been circulated and discussed in their absence. Introducing the code during a period of unrest and insecurity among employees can also be undesirable. If a code is introduced during a time of mass redundancies, the organisation runs the risk that the code is seen in the wrong light. Emotions can run very high, especially if the code sets out what the organisation offers its employees or if it sets down strict rules and regulations. 'Not only am I robbed of my function, but also my freedom to act,' said one employee when his company introduced a very restrictive code during a drastic reorganisation. Obviously one should avoid 'one of these days' becoming 'none of these days'. It is certainly true that managers dreading the introduction of the code keep finding excuses to postpone it.

Seek out regular moments to communicate the code

Without periodically paying attention to the code, it will fade away over time. The code is not a perpetual mobile which once activated will remain in motion. After relatively intensive attention during the introduction, it is desirable to communicate the code regularly. This can take place at fixed times, such as during performance reviews, New Year speeches and during quarterly reports; this will be discussed in more detail in the following chapter. There is also an art in finding new moments to surprise employees and prompt them to think about the code. The number of communication opportunities strongly depends on the introduction. Organisations can introduce their code gradually or with a shock. In the first case, communication takes place in digestible parts over time whereby it is gradually integrated as a normal component of business conduct. In the second case, much communication and activity take place over a short period of time, which quickly and urgently focuses everyone's attention. The type of communication also depends on the organisation's choice to communicate the code independently or as part of other programmes. The advantage of the first approach is that it receives special attention while the advantage of the second approach is that the code is not seen as separate but as part of other measures and activities of the organisation.

Check regularly whether the code needs modification or clarification

A code is never final or complete; it is a living document requiring adjustment and readjustment. The factors discussed in Chapter 3 are all subject to change. Expectations of stakeholders and society can change. New issues can arise. Laws can be tightened and judges can pronounce new verdicts. New branches in new locations can be opened and new employees, new products and new markets can be developed. Such developments often have implications for a code and its meaning. The organisation should therefore remain alert and where necessary reformulate parts of the code. This requires openness towards the outside world. Some organisations have amended their code three times in ten years. There are also organisations that update their code at predetermined points in time because recasting the code offers an opportunity to put it back on the agenda.

Good role-modelling behaviour: set an example and demonstrate vision

Second, leadership is about good role-modelling behaviour. What are the relevant points of interest in this regard?

Communicate a strong and personal message regarding the importance of the code

Management is credible only if the importance of the code is wholeheartedly endorsed. If employees feel that management is using the code as a public relations exercise, the code is meaningless. The inner conviction of management should be communicated in a clear and stimulating manner. Try to come up with a powerful statement of why, in your view, the code is important. Why is the code important to you? What in your opinion is the added value of the code? Why can the organisation not do without a code? And why are your proud of this code? In this sense the CEO of a pharmaceutical company launched the code powerfully by saying: 'I will never ask you to do anything unethical or illegal. I will not tolerate anybody stepping out of bounds. We're going to reach our goals, but we're going to do it right. I give you my personal commitment.'

Summarise the code in your own words

Convince employees of your intentions by summarising the code in your own words. Demonstrate that you have studied the code, that you take it seriously and that you know it from cover to cover. Your own summary also gives the text colour. It shows employees how you interpret it. At one company where I ran a workshop I asked each member of the management team to give his or her own summary. It soon became clear how diverse their interpretations were. One focused almost exclusively on the points he did not agree with. Another understood that stakeholders were discussed in order of importance. A third did not interpret the code in hierarchical terms—which was correct—but instead linked importance with concreteness: the more concrete an item the more important it was.

Make the implications for your own behaviour visible to others

A powerful way to communicate the importance of the code is to demonstrate the change in behaviour it requires. Managers do a good job when they make clear what impact the code has on their own behaviour, what its implications are and what is going to change (or has already changed as a result of the code).

Visibly adhere to the code

It is important that what is written in the code is also recognisable to employees. The more recognisable, the more valuable it becomes. The manager who demonstrates adherence to the code in word and deed sets a positive tone. Precisely because employees interpret the code of the organisation from the conduct of their manager, the introduction of a code should be reflected in the conduct of management. Managers often think that when they comply with the code they automatically set a good example. But, if good behaviour is to be followed, it must be visible to employees and interpreted correctly. What behaviour do employees observe in their manager and how does it come across? Does it strengthen or undermine the code?

Seek out opportunities to set the unexpected good example

It is doubly worthwhile if you not only follow the code but also show that you want to go further than the code requires. That you, as a manager, surprise employees and exceed their expectations: for example, by turning down a gift whose value is significantly below the agreed maximum. At the same time such situations should not come across as artificial, causing employees to respond with 'our manager also felt the need to show how good he can be'. It is important to remain natural and not to act a role. Often a new code does not signify a moral epiphany. A manager who claims to have been converted after reading the code must provide very good and convincing reasons to the rest of the organisation if he is not to be regarded as eccentric, suspect or hypocritical.

Avoid weak moments

It is important to follow the code as diligently and consistently as possible. It takes only one blunder, mishap or violation for the credibility of the code to evaporate. Incidents of non-compliance could be exaggerated and magnified by one's supervisors, subordinates and external parties. Such incidents also tend to linger both within and outside the organisation and can be an undermining factor in all well-intentioned initiatives a manager undertakes. Clearly, setting a bad example works against the manager. If managers become inconsistent in their adherence to the code, so will others. The question is then whether they are inconsistent in the same things or only in those matters that are to their advantage. Managers who lie to customers should not be surprised if they find customers and also employees lying to them. And managers who do not take the paragraph on being a good employer seriously should not be surprised if employees don't take the paragraph on the responsible use of company resources seriously.

Examine which role model is the weakest link and address it

Good role-modelling behaviour in an organisation is the responsibility of more than one person. Not only the line manager but also higher management and the board bear responsibility for the code. It is therefore important to think through who the role models are and what behaviour these role models display. The proverbial chain is as strong as its weakest link. Top management is quick to assume that if they set a good example the rest of the organisation will follow, while local managers often justify this conduct with reference to the reprehensible behaviour of peers. And local managers are also quick to assume that their good behaviour is sufficient, while employees often justify misconduct with reference to reprehensible behaviour at the top.

Display vision

Exemplary behaviour can come across as rather robotic if it merely amounts to following the norms and rules set out in the code. This is not to suggest that a manager with the attitude of 'just do it' is not laudable. In certain situations it is indeed simply a matter of managing: ensuring that the code is implemented. Leadership, however, requires more. Leadership also entails having a vision that places the code in a broader context: why the code is important; what value the code adds to the organisation; how the code links up with the strategy, identity and societal role of the organisation. There should also be a vision regarding the content of the code: its strengths and weaknesses and possibilities for further development. Vision is also needed in the process of the code: a vision of what is expected of employees; when the code is effective; and how to embed the code. It is important to display this vision to employees and even to propagate it among external parties.

Demonstrate that the code works both ways

Sometimes managers are very reluctant to introduce the code. They realise that the manager must lead but doubt to what extent they should do so. What authority do I have to prescribe to employees what ethics they should adopt? Don't I come across as pedantic and moralising if I teach my employees moral lessons? If I hold up the desired code, won't it boomerang back? What am I to do if my employees accuse me of being in the wrong myself? And can everything I say not be used against me at a later stage? Such questions cannot be a reason to postpone the introduction of the code. The anxieties of managers should be addressed by the manner in which the code is introduced. Managers should stress in their communication that what is expected of employees is also applicable to them. The code cuts both ways. Such an approach prevents managers from placing themselves above the group and raising all sorts of undesirable questions. Humility goes a long way.

Commitment: positive motivation

After clarity and good role-modelling behaviour the art of leadership in instilling a business code is to create commitment among employees. How this is done is discussed in more detail below.

Be aware of employees' attitudes towards the code

Employees can have very different attitudes towards the code. Their attitude determines in part how the code can be enlivened and subsequently kept alive. An analogy from the animal kingdom:

- **Eel.** The slick employee management cannot get a grip on: nobody knows what he stands for and what he thinks of or does with the code

- **Hedgehog.** The employee who feels offended and threatened by the code and as a result becomes defensive and withdrawn

- **Mole.** The employee who assents to and fully endorses the code but who furtively seeks out creative routes to dig holes in it

- **Parrot.** The employee who repeats what is said in the code and does what it asks, but who takes no further initiative or expresses any opinion

- **Polar bear.** The employee who does not respond to the code and is indifferent, distant and cold (and growls at best)

- **Puppy.** The employee who is wildly enthusiastic and embraces the code unquestioningly

- **Raptor.** The employee who uses the code to seize every opportunity to criticise the organisation, to damage others and to cause problems

- **Sheep.** The employee who docilely follows the herd and is led by those around him; compliance with the code depends on what others are doing

So the question is: what types of employee do you have in your team? What will be their attitude when the code is introduced? Or what is their attitude towards the existing code? How do you deal with their attitude? What works well and what should be improved?

Emphasise mutual interest in the code

Compliance with the business code must be experienced as being in the mutual interest of the organisation and employees. Management must be able to show why the code is important to the organisation. But management must also make employees realise that it is in their interest: the code protects employees against themselves, is good for the atmosphere at work, leads to better and more rewarding relationships with stakeholders and promotes the personal and professional development of employees.

Emphasise the responsibility of each employee

Employees should be thoroughly aware not only of the importance of the code, but also their vital role and responsibility in realising the code in practice. Each employee bears responsibility for the code. They embody the code in their conduct within and outside the organisation. And everywhere where they encounter other people, interests or resources they give content to the code. Just one employee violating the code once can bring the entire organisation into disrepute. It is important that the code is viewed as both a shared and an individual responsibility for every person in the organisation.

Entrust confidence

Negative incidents often give rise to the introduction of a code or refocus attention on a code already written. The danger here is that management starts to treat employees as potential criminals. Threatening language accompanies the introduction of the code: 'It's your own fault that we have a code', 'enough is enough', and 'the days of fooling around are long gone'. Such an approach fails to appreciate the sense of responsibility and good intentions of the majority of employees in the average organisation. In order to trust employees they must also be entrusted with confidence. It is therefore important that employees view the code as a sincere attempt by the organisation to ensure that all employees act responsibly instead of an attempt to create a convenient back door to dismiss employees and keep management's hands clean in the event an incident occurs. If there are employees who cannot and will never be trusted, this problem needs to be addressed first before proceeding with the vast majority.

Emphasise the role of conscience and common sense

Resistance against the introduction of the code often arises from the concern that the code conflicts with employees' personal conscience and common sense. It is therefore sensible to frequently point out that the code is not a replacement, but rather a supplement, to personal conscience and common sense. Continued critical and independent thinking should be encouraged. But that alone is not enough either.

Focus less on incidents and more on inspiring areas for improvement

As mentioned before, incidents can give rise directly to the development of a code. Incidents can fulfil the important role of wake-up call. It is a concrete and undeniable manifestation of the importance of having a code. Clients therefore often ask me to create an overview of their recent incidents in order to clarify the business case for a code for them. Care must, however, be taken not to focus solely on incidents from the past. The idea is to look ahead. It is therefore necessary to formulate a shared ideal which people believe in and which inspires and motivates them. People are motivated and enthused if they can identify with the state of affairs envisioned. The more people are able to envision this state of affairs the more energy and drive it generates. Working on a code because of previous incidents means being driven by pain and guilt (negative motivation). Working on a code from the basis of goals and ideals means being driven by satisfaction, pride and even pleasure (positive motivation).

Enquire about people's commitment

An enormous energy boost can be generated by giving employees the opportunity to voice their commitment to the code. Giving people the opportunity to voice their concerns and objections avoids all sorts of ifs and buts at a later stage. Ask employees what they truly think of the code. Don't accept platitudes and vague answers. Be aware of their objections and engage with them. Even if the organisation already has a code it is advisable to enquire about employees' commitment to it on a regular basis. For example, during a performance review you can ask what their opinion of the code is and to what extent it is a helpful instrument in their own work. The question is what should one do if one or more employees are not willing to accept the code. The answer to this question depends on the extent to which their opinions conflict with the code and the number of people who share those opinions. Ultimately, an organisation that takes itself and its code seriously won't be able to tolerate a situation where employees—after discussion—cannot accept the fundamentals of the code.

Feasibility: make compliance possible

If the code is to be complied with, the organisation must create the conditions to make this possible. If the code is to be realisable managers and employees should have sufficient means at their disposal. What does this imply for leadership?

Conduct a periodical risk analysis

A code is often violated because people feel pressurised and because the opportunity presents itself. It is therefore important to know where the areas of tension and temptation lie, how great these are and to what extent they can be resisted. There can also be structural obstacles making adherence to the code impossible. Determine on a regular basis where there are potential risks, how real these risks are and what the consequences may be. For example, a company that claims to accept supply-chain responsibility, but fails to screen suppliers, runs the risk of contracting with questionable suppliers with potentially serious consequences.

Be aware of everybody's limits

Different employees deal differently with pressure, temptations and obstacles. One is better able to resist temptation than the other. A thorough understanding of the risk of violations not only requires that managers know the organisation but also their people. Be aware of individuals' limits. Be aware of the pressure each can bear. Be aware what each does when the pressure or temptation gets too much. How readily will employees go along with unacceptable requests from clients? How readily will employees take a short cut to meet targets? And how readily will employees play political games when their promotion to a much-desired new function is threatened?

Put a set of measures in place

A risk analysis offers an overview of weaknesses in the organisation. On the basis of such an analysis, required measures and activities can be identified. Take particularly those measures that limit the greatest risks. A host of measures may be required especially when the code is introduced for the first time. Ultimately a code cannot stand alone; it needs to be embedded throughout the organisation. The divergent measures and activities available will be discussed in the next chapter.

Improve the organisation with 'quick wins' and introduce more complex measures gradually

A crucial question in putting measures in place regards timing and phasing. Adjusting the organisational structure before disseminating the code sends a clear message that the code is not without obligations and that it has real consequences for the organisation. At the same time, it can also require far-reaching and time-consuming changes which can delay the introduction of the code considerably. One could also ask whether everything within the organisation should be straightened out at once or whether it cannot be done more gradually. Will the organisation address each discrepancy between norm and practice immediately and completely? Or does it opt to make small improvements for each and everything that should be improved or to identify a few hot topics and focus on them completely? The first route has the disadvantage of the organisation overreaching itself; employees see little progress and the endeavour flounders prematurely. The second approach has the disadvantage of creating the impression among employees that the code is being narrowed down to the selected areas of key concern. A solution to this problem is to take measures that will result in a few 'quick wins', where substantial improvements can be achieved in a short space of time, and to adopt a more gradual approach in dealing with the more difficult-to-manage risks.

Avoid conflicting signals

Each manager should be alert to ambiguous conduct. A statement such as 'I don't care how you do it, just make sure we get that order' appears to be a licence, even an order, to act in a questionable or even illegal manner if necessary. It is also quite fatal if a manager concludes a workshop on the code with the words: 'Right, let's get on with the real work', suggesting that the code is something separate to everyday work. Therefore, avoid using undermining signals in your verbal and non-verbal communication.

Develop individual skills and capacities

Not only should the organisation be capable of abiding by the code, each person should be able to as well. To comply with the code, employees must possess the relevant skills and capacities. If not, skills and capacities will need to be improved. If a code states that procurers may not accept bribes, the procurer should have the ability to recognise the signals of bribery and take appropriate action. And if the code states that employees should be service-oriented they should possess the capacity to think and act in a service-oriented manner.

Transparency: make compliance and its effects visible

Another requirement of leadership with respect to the code is to create transparency in the organisation. Transparency here particularly means making compliance and its effects visible. What guidelines can be offered in this regard?

Make achievements and improvements visible

For a code to be successful, its successes must be made visible. Showing its effects motivates and stimulates both internal and external parties. If people see that the code is alive and working well, support will increase quickly. And increased support will also lead to an increase in individual contributions and efforts to enhance the code's success even further. Make sure that positive effects are clearly discernible. In this regard, one company decided to introduce a code trophy. Each year an employee who puts the code into practice in an extraordinarily positive manner receives an award. Another company publishes examples in its monthly newsletter of what employees have done to make the code successful.

Engage with stakeholders

Not only is it important to make the effects of the code visible, it is often also advisable to engage with those parties who experience the impact of the code. Stakeholders become 'real' when they are given the opportunity to tell their story, communicate their interests and expectations, and voice their feelings and experiences. Scientific research shows that employees are less likely to treat stakeholders with disrespect if they meet them face to face.

Frequently check on the embeddedness of the code

It is advisable to keep a finger on the pulse regarding how embedded the code is. How is the roll-out of the code going? Which measures have been put in place? To what extent are the measures effective? To what extent is the code alive? And which ideas and suggestions are there to breathe new life into the code? By checking on progress, you and others stay alert. Ask employees about their experiences. And give them the opportunity to point out discrepancies before you proceed to offer your observations.

Monitor, especially what needs to be achieved

Where checking is ad hoc, spontaneous and varied, monitoring is structured, planned and systematic. Monitoring gives an impression of the degree to which the code lives. It's especially important to monitor what needs to be achieved. Too often, monitoring focuses on input: in other words, what is done to keep the code alive. Much more important—but also more difficult—is monitoring whether or not the code is in fact alive: in other words, the throughput and output of all efforts. In Chapter 10 I will discuss this in depth.

Set concrete and achievable targets

Monitoring is made easier if concrete, realistic and measurable targets are set in advance. This gives direction to monitoring and avoids later discussion about whether the correct things were monitored.

Do not be too hasty in reporting to the outside world

In their enthusiasm managers can be too quick to report the first successes of the code to their superiors and the outside world. So long as these are presented as initial successes this is fine. One should, however, avoid creating the impression that the code is a complete success and fully embedded too soon after its introduction. Rejoicing prematurely can arouse suspicion and lead to misunderstandings and dissatisfaction. Many companies therefore first take time to make a number of improvements before the status of the code is communicated to external stakeholders.

Discussability: acknowledge dilemmas and discuss them

A sixth important leadership challenge is to make the code discussable and keep it that way. In this regard it is especially important to acknowledge actual and potential dilemmas and to discuss them on a regular basis.

Create an overview of your own dilemmas

A code does not prevent dilemmas from arising. Indeed, a code often accentuates dilemmas. Dilemmas are conflicts in the code, conflicts between the code and business practice or conflicts in business practice. Dilemmas are important moments because they demand a decision on how to apply the code. Such decisions can work out well or they can lead you to take the wrong turn. For this reason it is important to be aware of your own dilemmas.

Periodically enquire after employees' dilemmas

It is just as important to be aware of the types of dilemma employees face. On average two-thirds of the dilemmas employees are confronted with are unknown to their supervisor. This can be done in a fairly straightforward manner. 'Which issues, tensions, conflicts or inconsistencies do you confront in adhering to the code?' Asking employees this question sends the signal that their dilemmas are relevant.

Utilise dilemmas as building blocks

Dilemmas are the touchstones of the code. A dilemma is a dilemma precisely because the code is at stake. The code is put to the test. Do people act in accordance with the code? Does the code offer a secure enough footing? By asking about people's dilemmas an impression is obtained of the situations in which the code could be compromised. My experience is that when people start discussing concrete dilemmas the code truly comes alive. It is by looking at the code from the perspective of dilemmas that the value of the code is revealed. What does the code say about my dilemmas? Does the code help me to deal better with my dilemmas?

Analyse dilemmas to the bone

To understand dilemmas it is crucial not to be too quick to draw conclusions. People's presentation of dilemmas is often incomplete: they often assume or omit certain facts or make other misguided assumptions. It is therefore important to postpone conclusions and keep on questioning until the dilemma is fully understood. Why is it a dilemma? Where does the tension lie? Why is there tension? Which parties are involved? Which elements of the code are in conflict with each other? Is it an isolated dilemma or is it connected to other dilemmas?

Do not solve dilemmas immediately

Entrepreneurial managers are often inclined to see dilemmas as problems that should be solved as quickly as possible. That's what one is meant to do with problems: solve them. Real dilemmas, however, are often problems that can't simply be solved. It would not do justice to a situation which is characterised by a conflict between equally important principles, responsibilities, values and norms. One could even say that real dilemmas cannot be solved: whatever you do, it won't be completely right. For this reason dilemmas should not be seen as a sign of weakness in the sense that the person facing the dilemma failed to think matters through properly (which would have prevented the dilemma from arising), that he or she failed to adequately examine how to solve the dilemma, or that he or she is incapable of making a decision that would dirty their hands. Delaying a decision can be a sign of strength: wanting to come to a well-considered decision and to give others the opportunity to make suggestions and share their views.

Share your personal dilemmas with others

If you want employees and colleagues to share their dilemmas with you, it is important that you share yours. Discussing a personal dilemma with others need not be a sign of weakness. Taking a vulnerable position may be appreciated because it shows the truly problematic nature of dilemmas and that the code simply does not make provision for it. It is precisely then that one has the opportunity to discuss the content and the meaning of the code, but also its limitations and other reasonable and acceptable norms and values that play a role in decision-making. There is in this respect no better 'training on the job' regarding the code than discussing personal dilemmas in your team and relating each dilemma to the code.

Do not avoid debate

Dialogue is often the best way to explore dilemmas properly. If everyone's perspective is respected, thoughts can be openly exchanged. This does not mean that discussions should be meek and mild. Sparks may certainly fly in discussions about dilemmas. After all, friction generates heat. When people are allowed to show their emotions, their involvement intensifies. When people are allowed to pour out their heart, truths are revealed and matters become discussable which would otherwise be cloaked in labels, duty and courtesies. A debate with daggers drawn can therefore be enriching.

Teach employees to weigh dilemmas independently

A code is not an answer to all problems and dilemmas. Dilemmas remain. For this reason it is important to provide employees with tools to assist them in engaging with dilemmas. What steps do you take when you are confronted with a dilemma? What information do you collect? How do you define the interests and moral expectations that are at stake? How do you arrive at a decision? And how do you communicate the decision?

Eradicate rationalisations

Rationalisations, arguments that justify violations of the code before or after they are committed, are deadly for a code. Such rationalisations can be deeply entrenched in organisational culture. Common rationalisations include:

- 'Violating the code just once is not that bad'

- 'Everyone has violated the code once'

- 'The code is only for goody-goodies'

- 'The code is only for employees with criminal intentions'

- 'The code is just a paper tiger'

- 'Ultimately, I am the one who determines what is right and wrong'

Communicate not only the decision but also the reasons behind it

A code is meant to add a new perspective in the decision-making process but not to offer ready-made answers. It is therefore important to indicate the role the code played in reaching important decisions. Others will see how the code works and what role it played in reaching a responsible decision.

Discuss the code periodically

A code that is not regularly a topic of discussion becomes a dead letter. The existence of a code does not mean that questions and uncertainties have been banished from the organisation. Indeed, employees only become more alert and ask more questions. A code cannot possibly have a clear answer to every possible situation. Grey areas remain. How do I ensure that the code remains discussable? How do I ensure that it is discussed continuously? Communicating a code by decree does not work. In this regard the question is how explicitly the code should be brought up for discussion. The more explicit the attention, the more the code will be seen as an autonomous and independent instrument. The more implicit the attention, the more employees will view it as an integral part of their work. Some organisations ask their divisions to make the code a topic of discussion once a year which could create the impression that the duty of the divisions towards embedding the code is thus fulfilled. On the other hand, special attention to the code can create an opportunity to discuss matters that are otherwise neglected. Is the code still current? Which parts of the code are the most difficult to realise in practice? Which obstacles to adhering to the code are encountered within the organisation? Which supplementary activities should we develop?

Share dilemmas with external stakeholders

It is not only important to discuss the code and related dilemmas with employees. External stakeholders can also be involved. Discussing the dilemmas the organisation is confronted with cultivates understanding for the issues at hand and provides an opportunity for others to offer potential solutions.

Enforcement: show appreciation where possible and impose punishment where necessary

The seventh and final condition of a living code is enforcing it. And leadership is needed here as well. Good leadership will show appreciation to employees who comply with the code despite pressures to avoid and undermine the code. Leadership will also address alleged breaches of the code and impose sanctions where necessary.

Act immediately on signals of alleged violations

If the code is taken seriously, employees who intentionally violate the code should be called to account for their conduct. Tolerating violations undermines the code: it shows that—in the end—other interests and considerations are more important. Making allowances for a violation once is irreversible and invites further violations, from both those whose conduct is not corrected and from those who were aware of it. The idea that 'if others are not punished, I will also get off scot-free' quickly takes hold. And at that moment the code is at risk. For this reason it is sometimes good that a violation occurs. By imposing sanctions management demonstrates that the code is taken seriously and that non-compliance has real consequences. It is especially important that management acts decisively and thoroughly in the event that violations occur. Too often managers adopt a wait-and-see attitude, fearing that they may burn their fingers, make a mistake and or even be tarred by the problem themselves. Don't hesitate when signals crop up, examine the facts and then let the facts speak for themselves.

Not every violation is equally serious

Once it's been determined that a transgression has taken place it is vital to impose sanctions and take appropriate measures. It is also important to examine to what extent the individual and the organisation are respectively responsible. With reference to the seven conditions for a living code, one can determine whether and in what sense the organisation itself was at fault. In addition to taking into account mitigating circumstances it is necessary to establish the seriousness of the transgression. Not every violation is, after all, equally serious. Failing to achieve an ambition is less blameworthy than a clear violation of a rock-bottom minimum standard.

Dare to declare someone's innocence

Often managers are more willing to declare someone guilty than to declare them innocent. It is after all much easier to state what someone is than what they're not. It is however very damaging if unfounded rumours about transgressions are not refuted. Such rumours continue to fester and grow. Not only does it affect the atmosphere within the organisation but it also undermines the credibility of those who are accused of wrongdoing. Management makes a powerful impression if such rumours are quashed and tackled at the root, thus preventing people from becoming the victims of backbiting and slander.

Show appreciation for people who report themselves

Incidents will not disappear entirely because you have a code. For this reason it is important that such incidents are reported as quickly as possible. Employees who overstep the mark deserve a good talking-to. At the same time employees deserve recognition if they report themselves. It remains more desirable that employees report their own misconduct and show regret than they hide their transgressions in the hope that no one will find out. In all cases employees must not be given the impression that as long as they report their transgression they will not attract sanctions. At the most, self-reporting should lead to leniency.

Learn from violations and near violations

An important characteristic of an organisation with a living code is that lessons are learned from violations and near violations. By learning from violations and putting appropriate measures in place, organisations demonstrate that they want to reduce the risk of violations reoccurring.

Seven lessons for leaders

In this chapter a range of guidelines for leadership to promote the living code were discussed. Table 8.1 gives an overview of the most important lessons in this chapter. To apply them in practice you have to ask yourself to what extent you (a) subscribe to, and (b) have already realised these lessons. By subtracting the figure in the second column from the figure in the first you will see where your challenges lie: the higher the figure the more important it is to start working on it.

	Endorse (1 = completely irrelevant; 10 = very relevant)		Realisation (1 = completely absent; 10 = completely present)		Difference
Clarity					
Memorise the code	...	−	...	=	...
Work through practical examples to understand the code better	...	−	...	=	...
Devote time to employees' first encounter with the code	...	−	...	=	...
Ensure that employees know the content of the code	...	−	...	=	...
Emphasise underlying values and responsibilities	...	−	...	=	...
Teach employees to translate the code into personal conduct	...	−	...	=	...
Make sure that the code hurts	...	−	...	=	...

TABLE 8.1 Seven lessons for successfully embedding a code (continued over)

	Endorse (1 = completely irrelevant; 10 = very relevant)		Realisation (1 = completely absent; 10 = completely present)		Difference
Clarity (continued)					
Ask employees about their own code	…	−	…	=	…
Point out the limitations of the code	…	−	…	=	…
Determine how flexible or rigid you want to be	…	−	…	=	…
Choose the right moment to introduce and communicate the code	…	−	…	=	…
Look for regular times to communicate the code	…	−	…	=	…
Check regularly whether the code needs modification or clarification	…	−	…	=	…

TABLE 8.1 (from previous page; continued opposite)

		Endorse (1 = completely irrelevant; 10 = very relevant)		Realisation (1 = completely absent; 10 = completely present)		Difference
Good role-modelling behaviour	Communicate a strong and personal message regarding the importance of the code	...	—	...	=	...
	Summarise the code in your own words	...	—	...	=	...
	Make its implications for your own behaviour visible to others	...	—	...	=	...
	Visibly adhere to the code	...	—	...	=	...
	Seek out the unexpected opportunities to set a good example	...	—	...	=	...
	Avoid weak moments	...	—	...	=	...
	Examine which role model is the weakest link and address it	...	—	...	=	...
	Display vision	...	—	...	=	...
	Demonstrate that the code works both ways	...	—	...	=	...

TABLE 8.1 (from previous page; continued over)

Commitment	Endorse (1 = completely irrelevant; 10 = very relevant)		Realisation (1 = completely absent; 10 = completely present)		Difference
Be aware of employees' attitude towards the code	...	–	...	=	...
Emphasise mutual interest in the code	...	–	...	=	...
Emphasise the responsibility of each employee	...	–	...	=	...
Entrust confidence	...	–	...	=	...
Emphasise the role of conscience and common sense	...	–	...	=	...
Focus less on incidents and more on inspiring areas for improvement	...	–	...	=	...
Enquire about people's commitment	...	–	...	=	...

TABLE 8.1 (from previous page; continued opposite)

		Endorse (1 = completely irrelevant; 10 = very relevant)	Realisation (1 = completely absent; 10 = completely present)	=	Difference
Feasibility	Conduct a periodical risk analysis	...	— ...	=	...
	Be aware of everybody's limits. Put a set of measures in place	...	— ...	=	...
	Improve the organisation with 'quick wins' and introduce more complex measures gradually	...	— ...	=	...
	Avoid conflicting signals	...	— ...	=	...
	Develop individual skills and capacities	...	— ...	=	...
Transparency	Make achievements and improvements visible	...	— ...	=	...
	Engage stakeholders	...	— ...	=	...
	Check frequently on the embeddedness of the code	...	— ...	=	...

TABLE 8.1 (from previous page; continued over)

		Endorse (1 = completely irrelevant; 10 = very relevant)	–	Realisation (1 = completely absent; 10 = completely present)	=	Difference
Transparency (continued)	Monitor especially what needs to be achieved	...	—	...	=	...
	Set concrete and achievable targets	...	—	...	=	...
	Do not be too hasty in reporting to the outside world	...	—	...	=	...
Discussability	Create an overview of your own dilemmas	...	—	...	=	...
	Periodically enquire after employees' dilemmas	...	—	...	=	...
	Utilise dilemmas as building blocks	...	—	...	=	...
	Analyse dilemmas to the bone	...	—	...	=	...
	Do not solve dilemmas immediately	...	—	...	=	...
	Share your personal dilemmas with others	...	—	...	=	...
	Do not avoid debate	...	—	...	=	...

TABLE 8.1 (from previous page; continued opposite)

		Endorse (1 = completely irrelevant; 10 = very relevant)		Realisation (1 = completely absent; 10 = completely present)		Difference
Discussability (continued)	Teach employees to weigh dilemmas independently	...	— ...	...	= ...	...
	Eradicate rationalisations	...	— ...	...	= ...	...
	Communicate not only the decision but also the reasons behind it	...	— ...	...	= ...	...
	Discuss the code periodically	...	— ...	...	= ...	...
	Share dilemmas with external stakeholders	...	— ...	...	= ...	...
Enforcement	Act immediately on signals of alleged violations	...	— ...	...	= ...	...
	Not every violation is equally serious	...	— ...	...	= ...	...
	Dare to declare someone's innocence	...	— ...	...	= ...	...
	Show appreciation for people who report themselves	...	— ...	...	= ...	...
	Learn from violations and near-violations	...	— ...	...	= ...	...

TABLE 8.1 (from previous page)

9

Measures and activities
to keep a code alive

In the previous chapter a number of guidelines with reference to a living code were advanced to assist in the introduction, implementation and institutionalisation of a business code and, if necessary, sub-codes. In this chapter the focus is on the concrete measures and activities that can be employed to give content to these guidelines. It is useful to keep in mind that the link between all these measures is leadership, which I will return to once more in Chapter 12. The measures and activities are subdivided into three clusters: (1) communication; (2) human resources policy; and (3) other measures. This chapter concludes with a short discussion on monitoring the effectiveness of a code. In the next chapter monitoring the effectiveness of a code is discussed in greater detail.

Communication

The code can be communicated to the target group in a number of ways. A few examples are listed below.

Internal communication

There are many ways to focus attention on the business code:

- Making the code and accompanying letters and emails available in the readers' native tongue

- Launching a separate intranet site, writing about the code in the internal newsletter or magazine, as a regular or occasional feature

- Displaying it on the information shelves with other business pamphlets and documents and making it available in frequently visited areas such as reception areas, waiting and conference rooms

- Always carry the business code with you, in your pocket or briefcase, or keep it on your desk

- Developing interactive instruments to make the code a topic of conversation: for instance, through a game

- Organising special events and training: some companies integrate this training in their regular management programmes. Increasingly, companies train staff from top to bottom

- Printing passages from the code in company diaries and minutes of meetings, salary slips, the staff magazine and/or as banner on your website

- Quoting the code in speeches (such as the New Year speech, business news announcements, anniversaries and/or staff gatherings)

Training

A few functions of a code training programme are:

- Gaining insight into the importance of the code

- Recognising the relevance of the code to individual behaviour

- Improving (exemplary) behaviour

- Recognising and dealing with dilemmas

- Offering guidelines for embedding the code

Training often varies in duration from two hours to two days. Training also varies in what is taught: knowledge (clarity), know-how (realisability) and/or motivation (commitment). E-learning modules are often focused on the acquisition of knowledge, role-plays with actors on the acquisition of know-how and visual materials on fostering commitment.

Work consultations

The code can also be put on the agenda of regular work meetings. This would involve discussing concrete daily issues that are related to the code. Potential objectives of such discussions are:

- Creation of openness to discuss questions

- Offering mutual support in engaging with difficult situations at work

- Reaching a shared understanding of the code and making work agreements

It can be useful to start such consultations with a discussion of a few general cases before moving on to current and specific problems and dilemmas. Such an approach is less threatening. The more realistic the cases the more employees will discover the practical value of the code.

Dialogue with stakeholders

The code can be put on the agenda of the works council, the supervisory board, the shareholders meeting and consultations with consumers and NGOs. Suggestions for improvements and additions to the code and/or practice could come from different angles.

Human resources policy

The code can also take in a prominent role in the human resources policy. A few examples are listed below.

Job applicants

The organisation can inform new employees about the code in different ways. It can form part of the:

- Job advertisement
- Information package for applicants
- Job interview
- Information package for new employees forming part of the employment contract
- Introduction programme, such as a discussion of the code with the new employee's line manager

The code can also form part of the pre-employment screening. As one director put it:

> We have principles and values. Everyone receives this when they are invited for an interview. We ask people whether they can identify with the code. If they can't or if they find it ridiculous we won't offer them the position.

One possibility is to present one or more dilemmas to applicants and to establish whether their response is consistent with the code. Tailor-made assessment programmes have even been developed for this.

New recruits

New recruits approach the organisation with an open mind. The company can learn a lot from them about its culture, existing practices and actual dilemmas. To find out more, the following questions can be asked: 'If you look back on your first months here, how does the code compare to actual business practice?', 'Do you think that the code is complied with in practice?' and 'In your experience, would you say there is sufficient space in your work to comply with the code?'

Signing

Signing the code can take place in diverse ways. In this regard, a distinction can be drawn in:

- The moment: on commencement of employment, once-only (on receipt) or periodically (for instance, annually)

- Who: everyone, managers (at a certain level) and/or employees in high-risk functions

- What: to receive, to see, to agree to, for retrospective compliance (having complied with it) or for prospective compliance (undertaking to comply with it)

Screening

Managers and employees in high-risk functions can—perhaps periodically—be screened on the code. Some organisations carry out background checks on their staff. Gambling and alcohol addiction, debt and close relations with people with a criminal background can pose a threat to the integrity of the individual and even the organisation as a whole.

Performance appraisal

A code provides criteria with reference to which performance can be discussed and assessed. It is conceivable that the code comes up for discussion only if there is something specific to be said about it. However, the code can also be an integral component of every performance review. Questions in the performance review could include 'Have you encountered any dilemmas in adhering to the code in the past year?', 'Do you think that the company puts sufficient effort into realising the code?' and 'Which aspects of the code do you have difficulty adhering to?'

Coaching

Managers and employees can also be offered individual coaching regarding the code. A coach can guide individuals in the resolution of dilemmas, in setting a good example, in dealing with pressure and temptations and in the effective enforcement of the code.

Sanctioning policy

The code is not optional. A human resources manager once remarked: 'If a company has never dismissed anyone for violating the code, the code is not alive.' Even though this might be true, the opposite is not (if someone has been dismissed for violating the code, then the code is alive). Equally untenable is the assumption that the more people dismissed as a result of violations of the code, the more effective it is. What is important nonetheless is that the organisation has an effective and fair sanctioning policy which sets out the procedure to follow in imposing sanctions and which specifies the penalty applicable to different types of violation of the code.

Exit interviews

An exit interview is a rich source of information about the effectiveness of the code. 'To conclude, may I ask you what you think are the greatest gaps between the code and business practice? And could you perhaps give concrete examples to illustrate this without naming any individuals?'

Other measures

In addition to measures and activities in the areas of communication and human resources policy there are also other areas in which activities and measures can be employed to embed the code effectively in the organisation.

Decision-making checklist

Some companies use a standard checklist in decision-making where one of the questions that has to be answered and ticked off is whether the intended course of action is in line with the code.

Code owners

A functionary can be appointed who bears specific responsibility for a particular topic that is covered in the code. This responsibility can involve following relevant external developments pertaining to the specific passage in the code, providing guidance in its introduction and implementation, and monitoring and maintaining compliance.

Administrative measures

Of importance in this regard are proper procedures, systems and structures that support the code. Administrative measures connected to the code include the clear separation of functions, rotation of functions, sound book-keeping, registration of sideline activities and a gift register.

Contracts

The code can also be included in contracts with stakeholders. It can be included as a whole or in part. By including the code in the contract it acquires legal status. It can exclude stakeholders who are unwilling to comply with the code.

Screening of stakeholders

Just like employees, external stakeholders can also be screened. Companies increasingly want insight into, for example, their supply chain: whether suppliers are, for example, complicit with use of child labour or are practising sound environmental management. The code can be an aid in this regard. When a code is included in a contract, screening on compliance is a logical consequence.

Risk analysis

A code risk analysis can be conducted by analysing per element what the risks of transgression are, the level of risk, how substantial these risks are and identifying supplementary measures that could be introduced to mitigate risks.

Safety net

Questions about difficult situations and signs of transgression of the code should in the first instance be discussed with the direct line manager. Employees, however, may not be able to raise an issue with a manager, especially if the problem is structural or if the manager is part of the problem. For larger organisations it is therefore especially important and legally even advisable or compulsory to establish an ethics safety net. Many companies have in this respect a compliance or ethics officer. Often a whistle-blowing and/or complaints procedure is desirable in order to establish clear guidelines for reporting and handling alleged violations. An investigative protocol that stipulates per infringement who should do what and which procedure to follow is also advisable.

Code commission or ethics office

A code commission meets on a regular basis to discuss issues and current questions. Employees can, for example, submit ethical questions, dilemmas and suggestions to such a commission of external and/or internal experts. An ethics office is often an internal consultancy bureau that develops a number of activities to stimulate compliance with the code.

Monitoring

To ensure that a concerted effort is made to realise the code in practice it is advisable to include the code in the standard planning and control cycle. The business code can be the basis for internal accounting (of employees to managers, of managers to the board and the board to the supervisory board) and for external accounting (to shareholders, other stakeholders and society in general). Reporting can take place monthly to once every two to three years, for the whole organisation as well as by each business division. The results can be audited internally and/or externally.

The board can conclude a management contract with the management teams of different divisions to make written agreements on objectives for the embeddedness and effectiveness of the code. A similar arrangement can be made between managers and employees regarding the integration of the code into individual annual plans. As shown in Figure 9.1, the following steps can be distinguished in the management contract cycle:

- Translating the code into spearheads

- Translating the spearheads into quantifiable objectives (targets)

- Putting agreements in writing

- Monitoring the realisation of agreements

- Reporting on the basis of monitoring

- Auditing the report by verifying information presented

- Management discussions on the verified report, assessing performance, dispensing rewards and imposing sanctions

- Making new agreements for the coming period (and starting the contract cycle again)

A few advantages to including the code in the planning and control cycle of each division are:

- The process is irreversible (it maintains itself which prevents it from disappearing)

- Progress is systematically monitored

- Reporting makes internal benchmarking possible

- The code is given the status it deserves: as an integral component in the appraisal of divisions and managers

FIGURE 9.1 Management contract cycle for the code

- It stimulates continuous improvement of business practice in line with the code

- It offers learning opportunities within the chain of command and other divisions

- The management contract and report constitute the input for an external annual report about the embeddedness and effectiveness of the code

- The development of spearheads, targets and indicators is a process that is undertaken jointly

- Such a joint endeavour fosters support for the systematic realisation of the code in practice

In the next chapter I will examine what measures there are to determine the effectiveness of a code. In conclusion to this chapter Table 9.1 gives an overview of the measures that the largest 200 companies in the world with a code have put in place.

Measures	Percentage
Auditing and monitoring programmes on compliance with the code	88
Incident reporting system	85
Distribution of the code to more than 95% of the staff	85
Policies to investigate and take corrective action if misconduct is alleged	83
Policies to hold employees and managers accountable for non-compliance	83
A confidential and anonymous hotline that employees and managers can use to report misconduct or seek advice	83
Whistle-blowing procedures to protect employees and managers who report misconduct	83
E-learning programme to communicate the code	81
Management training or information sessions on the code attended by at least 75% of managers over a period of three years	75
Management training or information sessions during the introduction programme	66
Written assurance by management or employees of compliance with the code	65
Screening of suppliers on their integrity	60
Strategic analysis on non-compliance risks	56
Employee training or information sessions on the code attended by at least 75% of employees over a period of three years	55
A protocol for managers should they detect non-compliance	55

TABLE 9.1 Measures taken by *Fortune* Global 200 with a code

(continued over)

Measures	Percentage
Background checks on prospective managers	53
An ethics committee that provides answers to reported ethics dilemmas	51
Official inclusion of the code in major decision-making procedures	46
Internal audit reports on compliance with the code for each division/business unit	45
Ethics as part of the performance appraisal criteria for managers and employees	44
Internal and external reporting on compliance with the code	40
Background checks on prospective employees	40
Reward and promotion criteria which are directly linked to compliance with the code	30
Code discussion during job interview	12

TABLE 9.1 (from previous page)

TRANSLATION INTO PRACTICE . . .

1. Which measures and activities in your opinion are desirable in order to embed the code in your organisation?

2. Which measures do you expect to be most effective?

3. To what extent is the code integrated into the planning and control cycle in your organisation? To what extent is it desirable to give your code a more prominent place in it? How can this be achieved?

10

How effective is our code?

A dredging company is under considerable fire in the media and from NGOs for doing business in a country where human rights are systematically abused. Indeed, the presence of the company is helping the dictatorial regime to remain in power. The company wants to continue operating in the country and sincerely believes that the population benefits from its presence. But it is having difficulty communicating its position in a credible manner. The NGOs and even a growing number of shareholders accuse the company of a lack of clarity, transparency and willingness to discuss its position. In an attempt to turn the tide, the company decides to develop a code which explains company policy. After four months, the draft code is ready and the company invites external parties, including NGOs, to discuss it in a number of roundtable discussions. During these discussions mutual understanding for each other's viewpoint grows. Because the meetings are always attended by a member of the board, stakeholders are gradually convinced that the company is taking the issue seriously. Even though the viewpoints do not grow any closer to each other, the code and the subsequent engagement with its stakeholders do help

to improve the image of the company. The public storm
subsides and understanding for the company's decisions
is gained.

The code of the above dredging company was a success. Its reputation
was enhanced and negative publicity subsided. How successful is your
code? How successful do you hope it is? And how can you know how successful (or not) it is? In this chapter a few elements present in a successful
code are discussed along with indicators useful in measuring the success
of a code.

Measuring points

The aim of a code is to influence the behaviour of an organisation, the
behaviour of its managers and employees and its relationships with its
stakeholders. In order to achieve this, the code has to be translated into
actual goals. Subsequently, indicators, preferably objective ones, must
be identified to determine whether the goals have been reached. If such
objective information is lacking, personal experiences will have to be
used to make an evaluation.

The code cockpit presented in Figure 1.1 (page 10) can be used as a
model to measure the success of the code. We start with the heart of the
steering wheel.

Seven conditions for the living code

First of all the presence of each of the seven conditions for a living code
can be determined. By measuring to what extent the conditions are present you learn how likely it is that the code will be complied with. You can
do this relatively intuitively. For each condition, the following signals,
statements and examples are relevant:

- **Clarity.** How often do I receive questions from employees suggesting that they do or do not understand or know the code?

- **Good role-modelling behaviour.** How often in the past six months have I set a visible example to employees regarding compliance with the code? And how often have I demonstrated clearly how I employed the code in taking a decision?

- **Commitment.** How many enthusiastic reactions to the code have I received from employees? How many critical comments have I received? What proportion of my employees has embraced the code and what proportion resents or rejects the code?

- **Feasibility.** How great is the pressure the organisation places on employees and is it compatible with complying with the code? How often do I receive signals that the work is getting (almost) too much?

- **Transparency.** How aware am I of whether employees are adhering to the code? How long does it take before I find out that an employee has violated the code?

- **Discussability.** How many times in the past six months has a direct colleague or subordinate presented a dilemma to me or my team?

- **Enforcement.** How decisive is the organisation in handling alleged transgressions? How many incidents have remained unpunished? And how many compliments have I given to people who complied with the code during the last six months?

The seven conditions for a living code can be represented by a ten-point scale ranging from a rating of completely absent to fully present, which can be completed quite easily. Figure 10.1 offers an example. When a condition is excessively present (as outlined in Fig. 7.3 [page 89]), this can be indicated by giving it a score higher than 10. The next step is to determine the desired situation, also by indicating it on the scale for each condition. The difference between your perception of the current situation and that desired is now visible for each condition.

A second way of determining the presence of the conditions is by taking a selection of recent transgressions and analysing them with reference

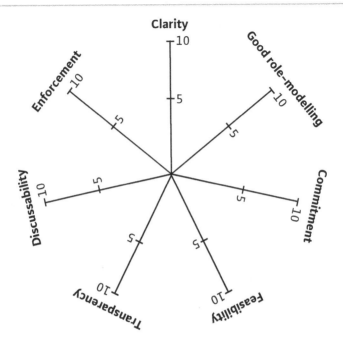

FIGURE 10.1 What is the current and desired situation?

to the conditions. Take for example the case of an employee who had accepted luxurious gifts. Did this happen because:

● The standards were unclear or unknown?

● Others in the organisation have done this before?

● The employee lacks commitment to the organisation, his or her work or the code?

● It is very easy to accept luxurious gifts?

● Earlier transgressions or temptations have not been signalled in time or not at all?

● Issues and dilemmas surrounding the acceptance and giving of gifts cannot be discussed internally?

● Previously discovered transgressions were not punished adequately?

It may be that specific conditions apply to each incident. But it could also be that there is a pattern underlying all incidents.

Measuring the conditions can also be conducted systematically by means of a survey. The *KPMG Integrity Thermometer* is a standardised survey that measures the presence of the seven conditions in the experience of managers and employees. A survey is an efficient measurement instrument that generates a broad and penetrating picture. In addition, it lends itself to follow-up measurements whereby one can achieve a fairly accurate overview of changes occurring.

Figure 10.2 presents the results of a company that distributed a survey among employees. The colour white indicates that the company scores better than others in the industry whereas black represents a lower score. This company scored well on prevention (the first four conditions). The detective and repressive dimensions (the other three conditions) were significantly less embedded in the organisation.

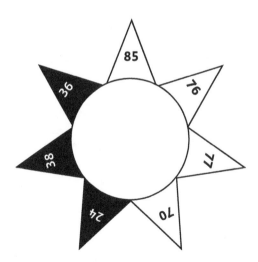

FIGURE 10.2 Survey results for the presence of the conditions for a living code (%)

Measures

The edge of the steering wheel concerns the measures that are taken to optimise the conditions for adhering to the code. First of all the measures that should be put in place can be identified. Subsequently, the extent to which these measures are in place can be established. Finally, the direct effectiveness of these measures can be determined.

One example is training employees in using the code. Step 1 consists of identifying the target group. Step 2 consists of examining who participated in which training. How many training workshops took place and how many employees have been trained? Step 3 concerns the quality of the training. What have employees learned? How did they experience the training received? What follow-up activities did the training lead to?

Such an analysis can be conducted for each measure. It is also possible to use an external or internal auditor to assess the quality and adequacy of the measures. A good auditor will approach this in a systematic manner. A range of methods can be employed: an analysis of documents (is the code, for example, properly integrated into other policy documents?), interviews with key figures (how is the code integrated into their work and how does it work?) and workshops with management and employees (what are the risks and weaknesses?). Tests and samples can be taken. Compliance officers or the hotline can be phoned with a fake report and the response time can be checked. The reports on performance appraisals can be examined to see to what extent the code was discussed.

	Existence	Implementation	Effectiveness
Training employees in the code	+	+/–	+/–
Code embedded in recruitment process	+	+	+
Safety net for reporting dilemmas and incidents	+	+	–
Procedures in investigation of incidents	+/–	+/–	–

FIGURE 10.3 Matrix of measures

The results can be presented in the form of a matrix indicating for each measure the extent to which the existence, implementation and effectiveness of measures is adequate. Figure 10.3 gives a partial overview of a company where such an analysis was conducted. Although many measures were employed and implemented, effectiveness was still inadequate because the implementation was ad hoc and unsystematic.

Effects

Ultimately embedding a code has the aim of bringing about desirable behaviour and outcomes. The dashboard in the code cockpit contains four meters. The first two meters concern conduct. A distinction can be drawn between positive and negative conduct, or between compliance and misconduct. In practice the emphasis often lies on misconduct: the less the better. Despite this being the case, it still does not mean that the code is being complied with in a positive sense. After all, a code often contains expectations of what should be done, such as creating a pleasant working environment, high-quality products and services, and protecting the natural environment. Measuring conduct therefore requires taking both positive and negative aspects into account. Accordingly, the dashboard includes the indicators 'misconduct' and 'compliance'.

The two other dashboard meters concern the impact of behaviour. Behaviour has consequences. Does behaviour translate into positive effects? Does it pay off? Two important effects of behaviour are on the reputation of the organisation and its financial performance, respectively the third and fourth meters on the dashboard. Reputation concerns the image each stakeholder has of the organisation. How great is their satisfaction, appreciation and commitment to the company? A number of survey instruments are available to measure the reputation of an organisation. It is striking that the code is often not very well integrated into these instruments. In this regard, it is not so much about posing literal and explicit questions to stakeholders about the code, such as 'Do you know the code?', 'Do you think we have a good code?' and 'Does the organisation adhere to the code?' It could well be that they do not know that the company has a code. It is much more important to integrate substantial elements of the code that are relevant to the company's reputation into the questions posed to stakeholders. If a company, for instance, devotes a whole chapter to corporate social responsibility, it follows that this should be included in research on the company's reputation by using statements such as: 'The company respects human rights', 'The company deals with the environment in a responsible manner' and 'The company is committed to improving society'.

A second important dimension of the intended effects of the code is its impact on financial performance. On the one hand this is about the limitation of financial damage. It concerns limiting costs as a result of:

- Theft

- Staff turnover

- Investigations of transgressions

- Dismissals as a result of transgressions

- Lawsuits and court cases

- Insurance premiums

- Compensation for damages

- Fines and punishments imposed by judges

- Erroneous decision-making (as a result of bribery, for example)

- Time spent on solving incidents and conflicts, both internally and externally

But a code can also make a positive contribution and increase turnover. The following positive impacts are examples:

- Higher-quality products and services provided by suppliers

- Better-quality recruits

- Higher productivity of employees

- Delivery of higher-quality products and services

- Greater efficiency and innovation

- Higher volume of sales

- Greater trust from investors and thus a higher share price or the provision of lower-interest loans

A qualitative evaluation

A code can also be evaluated in more general terms. In this instance, external and internal stakeholders can be asked what they believe the added value of the code is. For one company this exercise yielded the following positive remarks:

- 'The code is a means whereby taboos become discussable'

- 'The code functions as a driving force: relatively little energy generates a lot of energy'

- 'The code offers a framework for assessing and reassessing policy and each other'

- 'On the one hand, I would not be able to manage without a code any more. On the other hand, if the code were to be abolished tomorrow it won't make any difference as it is sufficiently embedded in our way of doing business'

- 'Unfortunately, I have had to part with two employees who did not match the spirit of the code. But herein lies the power of the code'

A few remarks from employees in this regard were:

- 'The code provided that little bit of extra encouragement I needed to report the transgression I had become aware of'

- 'I think the code is great because it creates an environment in which we can discuss matters of vital importance'

- 'With the code in hand I could show the supplier who tried to bribe me the door'

- 'By reading the code my eye quite coincidentally fell on a passage which made me realise that I had been unwittingly violating the code for a number of years. Since then I have improved my conduct and can now face myself in the mirror again'

Whether the code is effective depends largely on what the organisation regards as the objective of the code. It is the task of management to translate the code into concrete objectives which can subsequently be pursued. As mentioned in Chapter 9, such objectives should be as concrete as possible so that they can also be measured and monitored. Developing indicators to measure the realisation of objectives is therefore essential. This allows management to gain insight into levels of compliance and use the information to steer the organisation and account to external stakeholders.

The investment

The lever in the cockpit depicted in Figure 1.1 (page 10) represents the investment of the organisation in introducing, implementing and institutionalising the code. In a certain sense all organisational expenses and efforts should be related to the code. After all, if the opposite were to be the case, expenses incurred and efforts made would be undesirable since a good code expresses the desired foundation and direction of all behaviour within the organisation. Investments associated with the code are therefore often limited to specific costs involved in embedding the code. These include, for example:

- Costs of the ethics office, ethics officers and ethics safety net

- Total number of hours (multiplied by the average salary costs) that are spent on the code by managers and employees (such as communication, training and discussions)

- Time (multiplied by the average salary costs) spent on development, introduction and maintenance of specific measures related to the code (what is the cost, for instance, of screening suppliers, internal monitoring and the annual signing of the code by employees?)

- Total expenditure on advisers and auditors hired to assist with the code

An overview of the needed code-related investments can be created with relative ease. Knowledge of the investments (the position of the lever in the code cockpit) and their impact (the position of the steering wheel and the measures in the cockpit) offers insight into the output of the code. This output subsequently determines the extent to which new and/or other investments are desirable or necessary.

The real-time cockpit

To illustrate the feasibility of the code cockpit as a monitoring instrument, I now discuss an example of an organisation where the code cockpit was supplied with real-time information on the vitality of the code in each business division.

This case concerns an organisation that, over a period of three years, had employed large-scale activities to implement its code. When the integrity manager presented the code plan for the following year to the board, a discussion ensued regarding the desirability of the plan. So many activities had already been organised, why more still? Will we never be done with the code? The board gave the integrity director instructions to first measure the embeddedness and effectiveness of the code. On the basis of the results the board would take a decision on the follow-up activities.

With the support of a working group and KPMG, the integrity director developed a monitoring model that corresponded with the code cockpit as described in this book. Each division had its own cockpit. Likewise a cockpit was created for the entire organisation in which the information from the different divisions was aggregated. The cockpit as used in this organisation is an online system that can be accessed by the integrity director and management of each division to add information or for consultation. Figure 10.4 depicts the score of one of the divisions where the percentage indicates the degree to which the given indicator has been realised. Users could click on each percentage from their own computers and access other screens with background information and supporting figures.

The energy lever depicts the time, money and other resources that are invested in the integrity programme. In this way, a record of total hours

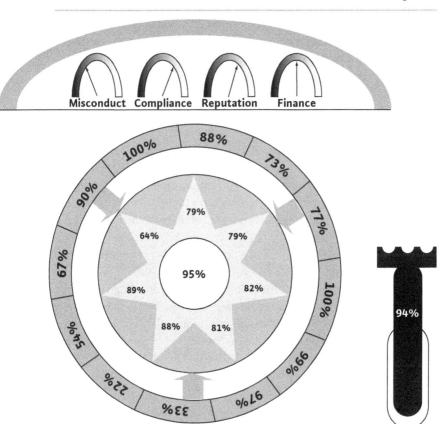

Figure 10.4 Example of the code cockpit for one division of an organisation

invested by all integrity officers is kept by means of an electronic time registration system which each officer has to complete on a weekly basis anyway. The pyramid and the star are measured at least once a year by means of a survey among employees. The pyramid is measured by getting respondents to interpret dilemmas and analyse whether the code is applied correctly. Each dimension of the star is translated into a number of questions and the questions that enjoy the highest priority are also accorded the most weight. The edge of the steering wheel is translated into 12 measures and the extent to which each has been embedded as well as its effectiveness is ascertained. The information required to determine this is obtained from risk analyses and test programmes that are conducted by the internal control department of each division. The dashboard meter 'misconduct' is supported by the electronic incident registration system where each incident is logged and each step taken in settling it is captured. Compliance is mapped largely by means of a survey among employees. To measure reputation a survey is conducted among stakeholders. Finally, the financial performance meter is supported by information on theft, damage, insurance policies, productivity and profits.

Because each division has its own cockpit, each can be managed in a focused manner. In retrospect, the discussion of the board was logical as eventually, from the information provided by means of the cockpit of each division, it turned out that embeddedness and compliance with the code diverged strongly between divisions. From Figure 10.4 it appears that the division in question was reasonably successful in meeting its objectives. With a score of 64%, enforcement scored the lowest of the seven conditions. Measures that attained a low score were awareness activities (caused especially by the fact that a large proportion of management did not participate), the quality of internal investigations of transgressions and the registration of gifts and sideline functions. Despite the relatively positive score on compliance and reputation, financial performance was average owing to the relatively high frequency of transgressions of the code. The board implemented the management contract cycle discussed in the previous chapter where, on the basis of the report by division, agreements were made with the management on targets for the next period. Prior to this phase in the cycle, the internal audit department checked the validity of each report.

The business case for business codes

At present there is a lack of conclusive scientific evidence to support the effectiveness of business codes. More than 80 scientific studies have been conducted on the effectiveness of business codes. Approximately half have found a positive impact while others show no impact, or even a negative impact.

One of the most important explanations for the conflicting results is that almost all scientific studies first established whether or not a company has a code and then linked it, for example, to the reputation of the company or the way in which employees engage with dilemmas. However, the effectiveness of a code does not depend so much on whether a company has a code, but much more on its content and the process by means of which it is established and embedded. Companies with a code cannot therefore simply be bundled together.

Many studies are also limited by mistaken conclusions regarding causal relations. For instance, if companies with a code commit more legal transgressions than those without, it does not necessarily follow that the code is ineffective. Companies that are confronted with a host of legal problems could very well decide to adopt a code which could lead to a decline in transgressions. The total number of transgressions could, however, still be higher compared with companies without a code.

Likewise it would be mistaken to conclude that a code is effective if companies with a code are more innovative and profitable. The innovative companies might be among those who developed a code at an earlier stage precisely because they are more open to new ideas and instruments. Companies with higher profits might also have had more financial means available to develop a code. Successful companies with high profits often have a prominent social profile and perhaps decided to develop a code precisely as a result of the societal pressure they're under.

In addition there is another extraordinary factor. While increasingly *more* companies have a code, this says increasingly *less* about the effectiveness of codes. The first companies that adopted business codes had one thing in common: the decision came from within. The code was seen as an important instrument, it formed part of the company ethos and the commitment from the company was more or less absolute. Today, totally different motives could play a role. Companies develop a code because it is legally required, stakeholders pressurise them or they follow the example set by others (the bandwagon effect). Having a code therefore may say little about internal motivation and commitment. As more organisations adopt codes, the average effectiveness of business codes could very well decline.

Research conducted within the Dutch and US working population found that a code has a counterproductive effect when it is introduced into a degenerate culture. In such cases, employees view the code as proof that the management is passing responsibility on to employees, that the code is a cover-up for existing questionable practices, or it is so far removed from daily practice that it is seen as a joke. A code can only be effective if the seven conditions discussed in Chapter 7 are present to a certain degree. The stronger the presence of these seven conditions, the greater the effectiveness of the code (see Fig. 10.5). At the same time, and this complicates the timing of the introduction, the existence of a code is also an instrument to enhance these conditions.

To determine the effectiveness of a code it is important to separate cause and effect and particularly to examine effects over time (longitudinal research). Most scientific research has little to say in this regard as the

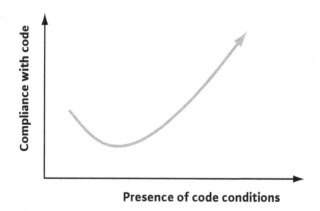

FIGURE 10.5 Effectiveness of business codes

research is largely conducted at one moment in time. And if it does say something it is mostly about the code's current effectiveness. Just as important, however, is the potential effectiveness of a code. Companies that have shown that their code and the related introduction process have been successful prove that a code can be effective. For this reason, I would like to give a few examples of these (partly) successful codes:

- **Damage (–24%).** One of the reasons for a transport company to introduce a code was the enormous damage employees caused to company property. Six months after the introduction of the code the damage had been reduced by almost a quarter

- **Absenteeism (–10%).** A manufacturing company used its code to bring diverse tensions among employees up for discussion. A number of causes for the high level of absenteeism became apparent and were subsequently addressed. Levels of absenteeism declined by almost 10% in the 12 months that followed

- **Procurement costs (–4.5%).** The procurement department in a large company noticed that its costs declined by almost 5% after the introduction of the code. Procurement rules were significantly tightened and suppliers were subsequently more critically assessed on their performance

- **Customer satisfaction (+31%).** Two years after the announcement of the code customer satisfaction at one car rental agency appeared to rise by more than 30%. Employees displayed greater receptiveness to the wishes, experiences and criticism of customers

- **Complaints about improper conduct (+100%).** Within a year after the code was introduced at a retail company, complaints about improper behaviour on the work floor more than doubled. After the introduction of the code victims clearly felt freer to report such misdemeanours

The last example preoccupies many companies: what is the relation between the code and the number of reported and confirmed transgressions? These companies are worried about introducing a code in case they are overwhelmed with employee complaints. I believe the life-cycle of code violations to be as depicted in Figure 10.6.

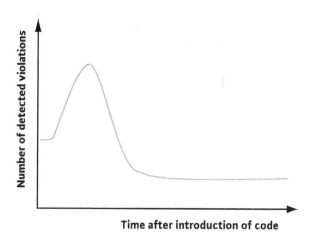

Time after introduction of code

FIGURE 10.6 Relation between code and violations

One could say that when the code is first introduced employees obtain: (a) a clear framework of the types of behaviour that are unacceptable; and (b) greater opportunity and legitimacy to raise alleged violations. This will clearly lead to an increase in reported violations. In due course, however, if everything goes well, the preventive effect of the code will become visible. A turning point is reached and a decline sets in: the number of violations will gradually decline. At the same time violations will never disappear altogether. The eventual more or less stable number of violations depends on the integrity of employees, the internal and external environment of the organisation and the standards the code sets. The higher the standards set, the greater the likelihood is that employees won't meet them.

Code life-cycle

Depending on the objectives of the code, its impact on these objectives can be very diverse. Every code has its own life-cycle. Figure 10.7 illustrates in simplified form six life-cycles that can be identified.

The rocket

Like a firework rocket the code ascends rapidly, explodes and after a short time it disintegrates. In the beginning the code receives a lot of attention. It is regarded as magnificent, but, shortly after the colourful climax, attention collapses and it ultimately has no effect.

The boomerang

From the start the code does not enjoy sufficient support among employees. The few who respond positively are enthusiastic when the code is introduced, but soon everything goes awry. The majority of employees see the code as a motion of distrust or a charade. Resistance grows because, for example, the code does not reflect the behaviour of management. Loyalty, commitment and trust decline further and the likelihood of transgressions even rises. The code backfires on its founders and has a counterproductive effect.

The empty shell

An enthusiastic start is made with the successful introduction of the code. However, following a crisis or incident the organisation loses credibility and support for compliance with the code evaporates. The code is like a thin layer of varnish, an empty shell, a cosmetic confection.

The early flower

The code is properly introduced and implemented and for a while also effective. But as a result of new projects and priorities the code disappears into the background. The organisation is also unable to maintain the

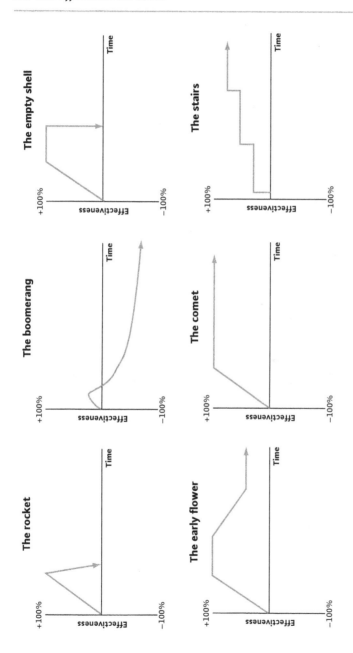

FIGURE 10.7 Life-cycles of a code

energy and originality of the code to keep it sustained. The code therefore slides back to lower levels of effectiveness. The code is still there but, like an early flower, it has largely lost its colour and aroma.

The comet

The organisation pays a lot attention to the code for a relatively short period of time after which periodic maintenance ensures that compliance remains at a stable level and attention does not fade away.

The stairs

The organisation introduces the code gradually so that business practice is aligned with the code step by step.

TRANSLATION INTO PRACTICE . . .

1. How effective is your code?
2. Which indicators do you use to determine this? How reliable are these indicators?
3. Do the indicators show continuous improvement?
4. Is further improvement required?
5. Which supplementary actions can I undertake?
6. What is the life-cycle of your code?

11

Personal accounts

This book has emphasised that a living code is one that provides meaning to people, offers guidance for business conduct and acts as source of value creation. It is important that a code appeals to people and inspires them. Three individuals have been asked to contribute their personal experience of working with a business code. What follows are the stories of a compliance officer, employee and manager.

The compliance officer

'Let me start by introducing myself. I have been working for my company for more than 25 years. In addition to different managerial and line positions, I have been secretary of the board of directors for four years. I have held the position of company compliance officer for three years. When I was appointed, I was given the task by the CEO to develop and establish compliance in the company. At the time no systems or structures were in place. Policies and standards of course did exist, but they were very outdated. In addition, their content was not aligned and implementation was uncoordinated. A few incidents, all of which received a lot of publicity in the media, made the company realise that these policies and standards needed thorough review.

'Given my background as a lawyer I started off by critically examining the individual policies and standards. First I collected every possible regulation that existed in the company. The rules for each country and division were often very diverse. In consultation with the board, I wrote four booklets: *Gifts & Entertainment, Insider Information, Customer Relations* and *Supplier Relations*. Each booklet had the same structure: an introduction which explained the importance of compliance followed by an overview of the relevant laws and regulations and finally what it meant for employees in practice.

'Six months after I started, the booklets were sent to each employee. In the covering letter the importance of full compliance was emphasised once again. We now had the same policies worldwide.

'And then there was silence. A disconcerting silence. I had expected an avalanche of questions and responses. But I only received a few phone calls and emails. At first I hoped that something had gone wrong in the distribution, but the postal services assured me that all of the booklets had been delivered to the 100,000 employees. The board did not appreciate my concern. Their reaction was that the booklets were so clear that they needed no further clarification. What more did I want? Compliments?

'Since I did not trust this conclusion, I approached a consultancy firm to conduct a survey to establish how the booklets were received. One hundred managers and employees were interviewed and the results confirmed my fears. Three months after the booklets were distributed three-quarters of respondents could recall receiving them. Half had made the effort to read one or more of the booklets. A quarter could reproduce some of the content. Only 20% still had the booklets in their possession. It was clear that the booklets had not had the desired effect.

'From the report of the consultancy firm, it transpired that there was nothing wrong with the content of the booklets. We as a company did, however, make a mistake in assuming that the mere dissemination of the booklets was sufficient. Apart from the fact that people do not read everything they receive, there are also other reasons why people do not take seriously what they read. In our case, people were not accustomed to headquarters telling them how they should behave. A broader framework within which to place the appearance of the booklets was also lacking. Many people also adopted a wait-and-see attitude. Due to the absence of any follow-up activity within the company, the importance of the content of the booklets was not properly communicated. From the perspective of employees, if the company did not take the booklets seriously, neither would they!

'I took one step backwards. I created a steering committee with the objective of developing a business code. The business code would be the umbrella for the booklets. The meetings with the steering committee were fantastic. I was not aware of the many issues and dilemmas people were grappling with. And I was also surprised how differently people thought about seemingly simple issues. The members of the steering committee became increasingly enthusiastic. At last we could talk about these matters. This led to an important discovery. If our discussions were so valuable and inspiring, it was our responsibility to create the opportunity for such discussions to take place throughout the organisation.

'Our business code ended up being quite concise. The most important principles could be written up in two pages. Each manager in the company was asked to discuss the principles with his or her own people. To assist the managers, we developed a toolkit with material to start up discussions and conclude them.

'And then we were inundated by a deluge of questions and requests. Managers in preparation for their sessions needed additional tips and information. Managers and employees asked how to resolve dilemmas they were experiencing. Since then I have been travelling the world to deliver training and workshops on the request of local management teams. The result of this endeavour is that "my" four booklets are very much alive. I have also received suggestions for improvements from all corners of the organisation. There have even been requests for booklets addressing other themes. What more could one wish for as a compliance officer?'

The employee

'Let me start by saying that I was pleasantly surprised by the request to give a personal account of the meaning of our business code. For me, the code had absolutely no meaning. I could therefore stop right here. However, knowing where this request is coming from, I have all the more reason to tell my story.

'It started about five years ago with the introduction of the business code. Each employee received an impressive booklet. The booklet set out the conduct which was expected of each and everyone. From the beginning I thought it was nonsense. And so did many others. We were committed to our company and we worked very hard. Why then should they suddenly tell us how we should behave? Apparently my manager shared our opinion, since in all these years he has paid the code scant attention.

'Until, that is, the day a group of forensic accountants announced themselves. I had to submit all my clients' files. A backup was made of all the files in my computer. And we were told that we were not allowed to destroy a single document without permission and that we were expected to give our full cooperation in the investigation.

'From that moment onwards things picked up speed. It wasn't long before I was invited for an interview to explain how I went about closing deals with clients. Who did I speak to, what sort of information did I disclose, how were prices determined and what did I do to persuade customers to do business with our company? A number of meetings followed over a short period of time. Gradually it dawned on me that I was the object of an investigation. As a sales representative I was very creative in attracting new clients. I organised business visits, invited interested parties to all sorts of events and entertainment and I was generous in the gifts I gave. On one occasion, I even had a discount deposited in a special account of one of my clients.

'The forensic report confirmed my suspicions. A whole chapter was dedicated to my transgressions. The company accused me of fraud and corruption and I was suspended with immediate effect. Dismissal followed shortly. My lawyer did not give me a chance to appeal. Not only had I broken the law, and here it comes, I had also violated the company code. I could not believe my ears. I worked myself to the bone for the company and did everything I could to acquire clients. And now I was being punished for it. Personal enrichment was after all not at stake here?

'On the intranet I found the business code. And there was indeed an entire chapter dedicated to gift-giving and entertainment. What I had done was without a doubt in conflict with it. Even payment of discounts to special accounts was explicitly prohibited. At that moment I sunk through the floor. How could I ever have been so dumb to ignore such a document? With hindsight I realised how terribly naive I had been. I thought that the pursuit of attracting clients was sacred, that everything else was secondary to it. That you understood your profession as salesperson well if you greased palms and lavished entertainment on clients. And that the company supported you wholeheartedly in it.

'Even though I am disappointed in my former employer and think that they should have done more to embed the code, I am ultimately responsible for my actions. I can only hope that my painful experience with a code is a lesson for others. Maybe it will be for you.'

The manager

'What my experience with our business code is certainly is a good question. And I think I have a good answer.

'I remember very well a long time ago when a headhunter approached me with the question of whether I would be interested in a difficult managerial role at another company. At the first orientation discussion the headhunter gave me a copy of that company's code of conduct. Fortunately, I was familiar with the code which was posted on the company website. It actually struck me that the code was prominently displayed on the homepage. The headhunter added that it was the most important document he could provide me with. At the time I thought to myself that an employment contract would be the most important document, but I also realised that the contract would ultimately be something between the company and me.

'But that was not the end of it. After I ended on the shortlist, I had an interview with the human resources committee. I had just seated myself when my eye fell on the pile of codes in the middle of the conference table. For the third time I encountered the company code. And, after brief introductions, the code soon became the topic of discussion. The chairperson of the committee mentioned that the company had grown thanks to a strong ethic which was established in their 'code of ethics'. One of the questions the committee put to me referred directly to the code. They wanted me to share my view of the code. They were especially interested in how I regarded the code as management instrument.

'My answer could not have been too bad as I eventually got the job. And imagine my surprise when the employment contract I received was accompanied by a copy of the code. In signing the contract I agreed to the content of the code and committed myself to complying with the code.

'Hot on the heels of the website, headhunter, HR committee and employment contract, followed a fifth experience with the code. In the introductory meeting with the CEO the business code came up. "Whatever happens, whatever you are asked," he said, "in everything you do, our *code of ethics* has to be upheld. Even if it is at the expense of our financial performance or in the direct interest of whichever stakeholder, we remain true to our code."

'The message has in the meantime become clear to me. The code was very important. I realised that the success of this company never exceeded the bounds of the code. Indeed, the success of the company is in fact the realisation of the code. As a start, I proceeded to immerse myself in the code. I read the content a number of times and repeatedly asked myself what it meant. I kept noticing new things. To better understand what the code meant to the organisation and to demonstrate my interest, I raised it during each introductory meeting with colleagues and employees in my division. I asked them the same questions that I was asked. How did they view the code and what did it mean to them? From the answers I was given, it once again became apparent just how deeply embedded the code was in the company.

'Now five years later I think that I have made an important contribution to the code. I have been intensively involved in the renewal of the code, I have dedicated myself to include the code in contracts with suppliers, I use it in screening them and I have made it my business to ensure that we now periodically measure compliance with and experience of the code both internally and externally. None of my previous employers had a code, and I have now discovered what a valuable instrument it is. Should I ever change companies I would either only work for a company with an equally powerful code or one in which I could make it top priority.'

The three accounts above demonstrate how differently people can experience a code. The account of the compliance officer demonstrates how a code can be discovered as an ethical framework for an organisation within which dilemmas can be discussed and sub-codes acquire meaning. The account of the employee shows how ignoring the code could become the grounds for dismissal. And the account of the manager shows how repeated and sincere communication of the code during interviews could turn someone who had no appreciation of the code into an ambassador for it.

TRANSLATION INTO BUSINESS PRACTICE . . .

1. Which of the three narratives above appeals to you most? Why?
2. How would you describe your experience with business codes? What is your narrative?

12
Leadership once more

Experience teaches us that it is leadership that makes or breaks a code. Leadership calls for insight, personal commitment and dedication.

Managers are thus required to reflect the code on themselves and their conduct. How do I convey the code in a convincing manner? How authentic am I in doing so? How do I guard against making mistakes?

To conclude this book, I would like to list a number of characteristics shared by managers who make a success of their code.

- They view the code as just a piece of paper but at the same time as the ultimate guideline for their conduct

- They know what is written in the code and what is not

- They are accountable and they also hold others to account

- They can articulate clearly what the code expects but at the same time they appreciate the dilemmas that remain unavoidable

- They are committed to fully comply with the code and they are at the same time flexible in its interpretation and implementation

- They ensure that the code inflicts both pain and pleasure

- They trust their employees but at the same time check and monitor whether employees comply with the code

- They appreciate conduct that is consistent with the code and they disapprove of conduct that deviates from the code

- They communicate the code in prosperous as well as difficult times

- They operationalise the code by setting concrete targets while at the same time not losing sight of the general objectives of the code.

Code-rich leadership is difficult but not impossible. Hopefully this book has succeeded in demonstrating this. And hopefully you have not been discouraged by it but rather been inspired to make a success of your code and your organisation. A successful code benefits your organisation, your stakeholders and yourself. Or, as Costco Wholesale states in its code: 'By always choosing to do the right thing, you will build your own self-esteem, increase your chances for success and make the company more successful, too.'

Does this apply to you, too?

About the author

Muel Kaptein has been active as a consultant and scientific researcher in the field of business ethics, integrity and compliance management since the early 1990s. He assists profit and non-profit organisations in developing, implementing and monitoring their business codes. He has developed business codes for more than 40 organisations. He has also developed a questionnaire for measuring the ethics and integrity of organisations, the so-called *Integrity Thermometer*, which is used by many organisations around the world. Muel co-founded the Ethics and Integrity consultancy at KPMG The Netherlands in 1996. He is currently director at KPMG Forensic & Integrity in Amsterdam.

At the age of 32, he also became professor of business ethics and integrity management at the Rotterdam School of Management, Erasmus University. He teaches courses in sustainability, leadership, corporate governance, management skills and business ethics. His research interests include the management of ethics, the ethics of management and the measurement of ethics. He has published scientific papers in international journals such as the *Academy of Management Review*, *Business and Society*, *Corporate Governance*, *Corporate Reputation Review*, *Journal of*

Business Ethics, Journal of Management, Journal of Management Studies, Journal of Organizational Behaviour and *Organization Studies*. He is the author of the books *Ethics Management* (Springer, 1998) and *The Six Principles for Managing with Integrity* (Articulate Press, 2005), and co-authored the book *The Balanced Company: A Theory of Corporate Integrity* (Oxford University Press, 2002). He is section-editor on 'codes of ethics' for the *Journal of Business Ethics* and board member of the Erasmus Institute for Monitoring and Compliance.

Muel has published scientific papers on the topic of business codes, such as:

- M. Kaptein and J. Wempe, 'Twelve Gordian Knots When Developing an Organizational Code of Ethics', *Journal of Business Ethics* 17 (1998): 853-69.

- M. Kaptein, 'Business Codes of Multinational Firms: What Do They Say?', *Journal of Business Ethics* 50 (2004): 13-31.

- M. Kaptein and M. Schwartz, 'The Effectiveness of Business Codes: A Critical Examination of Existing Studies and the Development of an Integrated Research Model', *Journal of Business Ethics* 17 (2008): 853-69.

Muel is married and has five children.

Index